inside bowling

don johnson

**with
jack patterson**

HENRY REGNERY COMPANY·CHICAGO

Library of Congress Cataloging in Publication Data

Johnson, Don, 1940 (May 19)-
 Inside bowling.

 1. Bowling. I. Title.
GV903.J63   794.6   73-6476

Published by Henry Regnery Company, 114 West Illinois Street,
  Chicago, Illinois 60610

Manufactured in the United States of America

Library of Congress Catalog Card Number: 73-6476

International Standard Book Number: 0-8092-8902-4 (cloth)

0-8092-8901-6 (paper)

preface

I'd like to share my theories and secrets on bowling in hopes that they will improve your game and increase your enjoyment of the sport.

Why? Because bowling has been very good to me, and I'd like to give something back to it in the form of instruction for its millions of fans.

Perhaps you'll never attain the degree of skill or the monetary rewards that I have on the Professional Bowlers Association tour. But I guarantee if you'll study and practice what I preach in this book you'll add many pins to your scores. How many pins will depend upon the degree of seriousness with which you approach the game.

Everything you need to know about bowling is included in text, photos, and illustrations, from the basics to theories for the high-average bowler.

I believe I am uniquely qualified to give you a total picture of bowling because I learned the sport from the ground up. I started bowling when I was 14 and have done just about everything connected with the sport, from menial jobs in typical family bowling establishments to competition under the white-hot glare of national television lights on the professional tour.

I grew up in Kokomo, Indiana. That's why I'm still called the "Kokomo Kid," even though I now live in Akron. Basketball was big in Indiana, but I wasn't tall enough to play. I weighed about 130 pounds, so I was too small to play football.

One day, I happened to watch the televised Championship Bowling series on TV. Here, I decided, was something I could do because it required no great physical attributes. I started going to the bowling lanes once a week when I was 14 to bowl for two or three hours. I was determined to become a pro. It wasn't easy. I wasn't a natural bowler. But I had desire.

When I graduated from high school, I went to work at Play Bowl Lanes in Kokomo, learning all I could about the game. I worked as a pin chaser, the kid who runs around unjamming the automatic pinspotters. After this I learned to be a mechanic for the pinspotting machines. Meanwhile, I always found time for 20 games of practice a day.

Later I took a job as assistant manager at C-Ville Lanes in Crawfordsville, Indiana. I did everything—scrubbing walls, working the desk, drilling balls, instructing. But I still found time for practice. I had a 165 average when I graduated from high school. By the time I was 21, I had a 214 average. That's when I joined the Professional Bowlers Association.

I'm sure the lessons I learned behind the scenes will serve me well when I settle down, retire, and operate my own lanes.

I've been through it all, as you can see. That's why I think I can give you insights into the game that few pro bowlers can.

Bowling is great fun, no matter how well you bowl. But if you can bowl better scores, the enjoyment increases. My goal is to see to it that enjoyment does increase as you absorb and master all that I am going to tell you in this book.

Don Johnson

Photos courtesy Bill Hunter, *Beacon Journal*, Akron, Ohio; American Bowling Congress; and Firestone Tire and Rubber Company. Photo on page 46 courtesy *National Bowlers Journal*. Diagram on page 58 courtesy Ebonite.

contents

PEOPLE OF ALL AGES . . . can bowl. My wife Mary Ann and her mother, Mary Baker, are both displaying excellent form.

chapter 1
TOOLS OF THE TRADE

Welcome to one of the most popular leisure-time sports in the United States. Over 52 million bowlers enjoy the game. In annual surveys, bowling is outranked only by fishing as America's favorite recreational sport. Its popularity is surging in foreign countries, too, particularly in Japan, Canada, Great Britain, and Scandinavia.

The beauty of this game is that anyone can bowl. Women can attain skills almost equal to those of men. Youngsters and older people can play, too. You don't have to be seven feet tall or weigh 270 pounds to excel in bowling. Some of the thinnest, fattest and most ungraceful people develop into good bowlers. Doctors endorse the game as an excellent form of exercise.

Weather is never a problem. You'll never get rained out in the modern, climate-conditioned bowling lane. Cost is minimal compared to that of other sports. Bowling fees are low, and the sport requires no mass of personal equipment—just a ball, shoes, and a bag in which to carry them. Compare

that with golf, where you need balls, nine-irons, four-woods, club covers, a putter, bag, shoes, umbrella, and golf cart—not to mention club fees.

Bowling is a speedy game. You can roll three games in about three hours, even in league competition. There are no long matches, as in tennis, or hours of waiting to play, as in golf. Bowling is a family sport. Mom, dad, the kids, and even grandma and grandpa can have hours of fun and relaxation on the lanes.

So let's get with it—to the equipment you'll need, how to select it, and how to make the equipment do the most for your game. We'll also look at some features of modern bowling lanes. Once we get you grounded, we'll move on to the art of rolling higher scores.

THE BALL

The ball will be your most costly—but most important—investment in equipment. The price will range from $20 to $50, depending on model, composition, and color.

It is impossible to become a good bowler without a properly fitted and weighted ball, one that complements your strength, physique, style of bowling, and even your personality.

A ball can last a lifetime, so it is extremely important that you exercise care in selecting it. The years of enjoyment and good scores the right ball can provide will make its original cost seem a bargain.

Plastic vs. Rubber

For years, the only type of bowling ball available was a black ball made of hard rubber. But in 1950 the American Bowling Congress (ABC), the ruling body of the sport, sanctioned use of a plastic ball made from a mold. The plastic ball opened new vistas in the sport. Plastic balls put color in the game. They can be produced in any shade. Some are speckled, mottled, even translucent. For fashion-conscious men and women, they color-key with attractive bowling costumes.

A great debate still rages over which ball —hard rubber or plastic—does the best job of knocking down pins. Some swear by the rubber ball; others think it already has been surpassed in performance by the plastic ball; still others say there is no difference.

For five years, I have used the plastic balls made by Columbia Industries, Inc., of Texas. I recommend you try plastic. I used a rubber ball for years before switching, so I've had time to compare. Besides, I'm in the pro bowling business to win titles and make money. If I didn't think the plastic ball did the best job, you couldn't pay me enough to use it. The greatest endorsement I can give the plastic ball is that I've used Columbia's plastic ball in 16 of the 20 PBA championships I have won.

For many years, Don McCune, Don Helling, and I were the only PBA tour players using plastic balls. Most of the pros were traditionalists and stayed with the black, hard-rubber ball. Today, however, more than 60 pros, most of whom are not under contract to promote any company's balls, are using the gaily colored plastics. In 1972, Mike Durbin won the $125,000 Firestone Tournament of Champions—bowling's World Series—with a caramel colored Columbia ball. The Tournament of Champions carries a $25,000 first prize—the largest in pro bowling.

Why do I believe the plastic ball is superior to the rubber ball? The plastic ball has a softer consistency, which allows it to skid farther through the *heads* before the ball starts to hook. The heads are the first 15 feet down from the foul line. This area is made of hard maple wood to absorb the shock of the ball. Farther down-lane, where the ball will grip and hook, the wood used is pine. The farther you can get the ball down-lane before it starts its hooking action, the better. The plastic ball does the job. It doesn't grip the lane and start to hook until it has skidded through the heads, perhaps 25 to 40 feet from the foul line. Using a plastic ball, you can definitely reach out for your *target* and hit it. I have no scientific data to prove it, but, personally, I feel a plastic ball is more suited to today's bowling conditions than is a rubber ball. The pins are plastic coated. Many lanes are finished with plasticlike substances for longer wear. I think plastic works better on plastic, providing a better *mixing action* when the ball strikes the pins.

Glenn Allison, a five-time PBA tour winner who is now a coowner of a bowling center in Los Angeles, told me three years ago that he was convinced the plastic ball carried one more *garbage hit* per game than did the rubber ball. By garbage hit, I mean

YOUR MOST IMPORTANT INVESTMENT . . . in bowling is a properly fitted ball. This "Swiss cheese" ball is what your pro will use to determine your finger size and finger span so a ball can be drilled to fit your hand exactly.

a ball that does not hit the *strike pocket* perfectly but still knocks down all the pins by explosive pin reaction.

I think the plastic ball snaps into the pins better at the end of a bowler's shot. That's where it counts. Many bowlers find that their ball hooks too early and is just lazily turning over by the time it reaches the pins. The ball deflects off the pins, failing to do its job of getting a mixing action. We pros call it *rolling out*—a ball fails to drive into the strike pocket and send the pins flying off one another.

That's my case for the plastic ball. However, you may find a hard rubber ball works best for you. Billy Welu, a great PBA performer and excellent instructor, contends that the hard rubber ball is the best for all lane conditions. Try both balls before you make a decision. No two people are the same and so, too, no two bowling games.

Weight

Once you decide on the composition of your ball, you must choose the best weight. Choose the heaviest ball you can control comfortably. The heavier the ball, the more pins you are likely to knock down.

ABC rules stipulate that balls must weigh between 10 and 16 pounds. For men, I recommend a 15- to 16-pounder. Women probably will be more comfortable with a 13- to 15-pound ball, but if they can handle the 16-pounder, they should try it. Junior bowlers, depending on their age and size, usually start with an 8- to 12-pound ball, which the rules allow them to use.

The best way to determine what weight suits you is to take advantage of the balls furnished free at every bowling lane. When you first take up the game, try several different weights. Find one you can control, one that doesn't make you feel awkward when you move down the *approach*. The ball shouldn't hurt your fingers or thumb or inhibit your delivery.

Then go to the pro or the proprietor of the lanes and discuss your findings. Your proprietor has equipment that will measure your finger span and dictate where the finger and thumb holes should be drilled for proper fit.

Do not wait too long before purchasing your own ball. You'll never be a good bowler if you must use a different ball each time you compete. Chances are that, at the lane, you'll never find a ball that is perfectly fitted to your game. Even if you should, what happens if you show up at the lane and someone else is using that ball?

If you don't have your own ball, you'll be bowling with improper equipment and your game will suffer. Experiment with the lane balls—then get serious with your own professionally fitted ball.

Color

I won't insult your intelligence by saying that the color of your ball will have an actual effect on the pins. But color can have a psychological effect, just as it does when you put on a new suit or dress. Color can make you feel better. You just might bowl better if you are rolling a ball of which you are proud and in which you have confidence.

Color is a major source of satisfaction in buying clothes, automobiles, and appliances. So why not in bowling? If a skyrocket red or baby blue ball turns you on,

by all means buy it, if it is the proper weight for your game.

A ball won't knock down a single pin more because it is brightly hued. But it could give you the psychological edge you need to throw the ball properly. And that's what knocks down pins.

SHOES AND BAGS

Like bowling balls, shoes once were black only. They, too, have come a long way in recent years and are available in all colors, styles, and sole types.

Your main objective in selecting shoes, however, is neither color nor style. What you want are shoes that are comfortable and provide a proper slide on your last step, when you are at the all-important point of releasing the ball.

If you are right-handed, the shoe you purchase will have a slick sole for sliding on the left foot and a rubber sole for control on the right. It's just the opposite for left-handed bowlers.

The sliding sole may be made of conventional leather, Teflon—the nonstick substance developed for cookware—or even soft felt. A manufacturer once developed a shoe with interchangeable soles to meet varying conditions on the approaches.

On the pro tour, I carry several pairs of shoes with me because we bowl in different lanes with different approach areas each week. In spite of this precaution, I didn't have the right shoe once in 1972. In the Waukegan Open I slipped and fell on extremely slick approaches and injured my thigh so severely that I had to drop out of the tourney when I had a good chance to win or finish high in the standings. So you see how important shoes can be.

I recommend a conventional shoe, because most of the time you'll be bowling in the same lanes and will be able to become familiar with the approaches. But if you find you have trouble with either too much sticking or sliding you may have to experiment with different shoes. You may not need new shoes. If you are sliding too far, go to a shoemaker and have him build the heels of your shoes up ¼ to ⅜ of an inch. If you're sticking, have him lower the heels by the same amount.

Once you get shoes and a ball, buy a bowling bag in which to store and carry them. Bags come in all colors, can be bought for a modest price, and will last a lifetime. The bag will have a large compartment for the ball and a smaller compartment for shoes and will keep both in top-notch condition when you aren't bowling.

CLOTHING

The only rule regarding clothing is to wear comfortable clothes that are not restrictive to your delivery, knee bend, and slide. When in doubt, buy one size larger. Double-knit slacks are ideal because of their stretching qualities. Women should not wear skirts that are too tight or short—there's a lot of bending and stretching in this game.

Millions of bowlers compete in league play and usually teams outfit themselves in matching uniforms. The most common team uniform consists simply of matching shirts, with each bowler's name on the shirt pocket and the name of the team on the back. Some teams, however, also wear matching pants or skirts. It is usual for businesses or organizations to sponsor teams for advertising or goodwill purposes, and often the sponsor will pay for the uniforms.

Personally, I like to stress being well dressed on the lanes. Bowling apparel comes in styles and colors to rival the beautiful outfits worn by today's pro golfers. My credo is: look sharp, feel sharp, bowl sharp. The modern bowling lane is no longer a smoke-filled cellar where tattered shirts and baggy pants are acceptable.

When I came on the tour in 1964, I was a "mod" young swinger. I had pointed shoes and a lot of unconventional but not stylish clothes. Eddie Elias, the founder of the PBA, made me see the light. He made me head of the PBA's image committee, which regulates not only the dress but the deportment of the pros, on and off the lanes. Although judging by today's styles I wasn't all that bad, some of the people watching our tournaments thought my dress was out of line. They complained, and I finally yielded.

I still consider this a mod, mod world. But I did begin dressing more like a champion and not like someone trying to seek attention by nonconformity. I still wear bright, modern clothes—but they are the latest in style and are always in good taste. I think dressing well helps my game and could help yours.

Johnny Petraglia, one of the top left-handed bowlers, sometimes wears shirts that have ruffled fronts, almost like formal wear. Barry Asher likes fancy vests. Dave Davis goes for shirts with large, ruffled cuffs. All of the pros have become fashion-conscious since they began bowling before big crowds and national television audiences watching in color.

Try some fancy bowling togs. I think you'll enjoy being well dressed on the lanes. Bowling attire today is so good-looking that you'll even want to wear some of your skirts, shirts, or pants when you aren't bowling. And when you know you look good, you'll probably bowl better.

THE MODERN BOWLING LANE

OK, you're decked out in your new clothes and shoes, carrying your professionally selected ball. What will you encounter when you go to one of the modern bowling establishments? Magnificence, that's what. Owners of bowling lanes have invested millions in their houses since the upsurge of interest in the sport after World War II.

The houses are so fancy you don't call them alleys anymore. Now they are lanes. If you threw the ball off the lane in the past, you threw it in the "gutter." But that's too vulgar by today's elegant standards. Now your ball goes into the *channel*.

Proprietors have modernized their lanes beyond recognition. An old-time bowler spit in cuspidors. Alleys then were dark and dingy, reeking of cigar smoke and sweat. Many were located in basements. There was a lot of cursing and gambling going on. Bowling alleys were much like the old saloons.

Today, entire buildings have been erected for bowling. Pinboys have been replaced by automatic pinsetters. The ball is returned under the lane so as not to disturb bowlers' concentration. The modern lane may have a restaurant, a cocktail lounge, and a nursery where mothers can leave their children while they bowl. The nonbowling areas are carpeted. Other features include piped-in music, plush lounges, and pool and ping-pong tables.

In Colorado, there is an "ultra-lane." A family can go there and bowl, swim, use the sauna bath, play pinball machines, shoot pool, eat a gourmet dinner, and retire to an adjoining motel for a family weekend. Mom can even get her hair done without leaving the building.

These "ultra-houses" feature 36 to 70 lanes to provide bowling without waiting.

A MODERN BOWLING LANE . . . is clean, sleek, and bright, with the latest technical equipment. These lanes are packed for the ABC national tournament, an event that attracts over 5,000 teams every year.

CUSPIDORS AND CIGAR SMOKE . . . have disappeared with the dingy bowling alleys of the past. The lounge in today's bowling house is a comfortable, relaxing place to rehash your adventures on the lanes.

Many are open 24 hours a day. It is not unusual for an industry to sponsor as many as 500 bowling teams as part of its recreational program. Many industries have their own lanes for use round-the-clock by shift workers.

In New York, there is a bowling lane that features Playboy-type "bunnies" who serve refreshments. This nightclub atmosphere sure beats cuspidors and cigar smoke.

The Pins

Hard-rubber black bowling balls, black shoes, wooden pins—all are being replaced, as the products of modern science find acceptance in the game of bowling.

Bowling equipment suppliers would have you believe a scarcity of woods made them switch from the conventional all-wood pins to plastic-coated wooden pins. Don't you believe them. Plastic-coated pins have more zing and more bounce. They mix and

fly more than the wooden pins of the past. The results are higher scores, happier people, increased profits, and lower maintenance costs. At $50 a set, pins cost the bowling establishment owner a lot of money. If the pins last longer, are more easily serviced, and provide higher scores, who can fault the owners for choosing the plastic-coated pins?

Even if you are only a casual bowler, you might profit by asking the weight of the pins used in the bowling house of your choice. On the pro tour, the pins are regimented. They are 3 pounds, 5 ounces to 3 pounds, 6 ounces. No pin can vary more than an ounce in weight in any rack of 10 pins. The pins in your favorite house might not weigh that much, however. ABC rules state that pins may weigh from 3 pounds, 2 ounces to 3 pounds, 10 ounces. Proprietors may choose any weight within those limits, as long as they make sure the pins in a 10-pin rack don't vary more than an ounce.

AUTOMATIC PINSPOTTERS . . . speed up today's bowling. Here's what the machinery looks like. A full rack of pins is always ready to replace the pins you knock down.

In tournaments, the pins could be heavy to provide tougher competition. In league and open bowling, they could be lighter to encourage higher scores. If the pins are heavy, you'll have to throw a stronger ball with more lift to topple them. If the pins are light, you may often get a strike with a less accurate but slower mixing ball.

I have no doubt that the plastic-coated pin of today has resulted in higher scores. But it bugs me when people say that today's stars of the game wouldn't have been able to cut it under conditions of the past. I counter with the fact that there are more good bowlers today than ever, despite a multitude of changing lane conditions created by heavy play. Just as there have been improvements in golf clubs and baseball and tennis equipment, so there have been advances in the game of bowling.

Bowling will continue to change as the pursuit of excellence continues. You must accept and master the changes and problems that will occur if you are to become, or stay, a top-notch performer.

BOWLING AIDS

In bowling, as in all sports, enterprising people have developed a variety of aids designed to help you master the game.

About 50 percent of the pro bowlers use some type of bowling aid, and only a few of them are being paid to do so for promotional purposes.

With over $2 million at stake in pro bowling purses every year, the pros would not use bowling aids if they didn't feel the aids were helping them shore up weaknesses in their games. However, any pro will tell you that, while an aid may help, the real key to higher scores is *you*. When your scores start dropping, 90 percent of the trouble is that you've forgotten a basic part of the game. In other words, you can

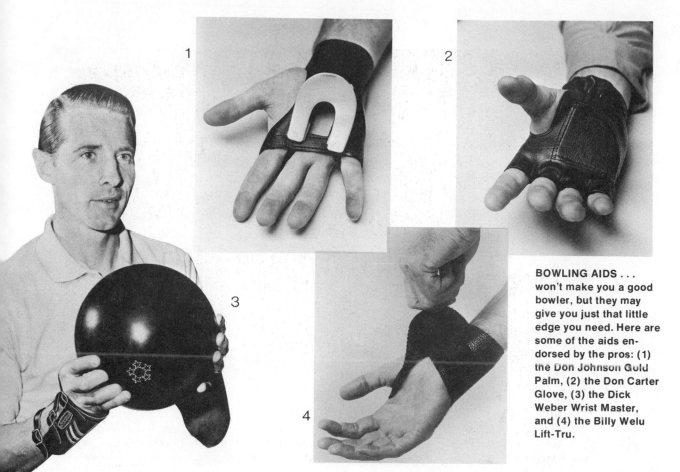

BOWLING AIDS . . . won't make you a good bowler, but they may give you just that little edge you need. Here are some of the aids endorsed by the pros: (1) the Don Johnson Gold Palm, (2) the Don Carter Glove, (3) the Dick Weber Wrist Master, and (4) the Billy Welu Lift-Tru.

try all the aids in the world and not get as much help in solving your problem as you can from a session with your local pro.

However, if your game is solid but you feel you are capable of scoring better, an aid might be just what the doctor ordered to turn a minor weakness into a strength.

The advanced or pro bowler thrives on experimentation, using anything that might raise his or her average a precious pin or two. I'm often referred to as the "Heinz 57 pro" because I'll try anything to get the jump on my fellow competitors.

Let me list some of the more well-known devices that have helped the pros. To the novice and intermediate bowler, I say: first, master the basic techniques of the game. You must have a solid game before even thinking about which aid might help you.

Gloves

I endorse the Don Johnson Gold Palm,

that strange device you see on my bowling hand in the pictures in this book. It features a plastic horseshoe built into the palm of the glove. The first time I tried it on (I represented another glove company at the time) it made the ball feel two pounds lighter at the starting position. The Gold Palm makes the ball seem lighter because it balances the ball on the three points of the plastic horseshoe. Unlike some gloves, it is adjustable.

The device can be moved forward to make you break your wrist more. If you move it back, you'll cup your wrist, causing more hook. Move it right, toward your thumb if you are right-handed, and you'll get more spin on your ball. Move it left, and you'll keep your hand behind the ball better at release.

There are three players on the Gold Palm staff—Earl Anthony, Allie Clarke, and myself. In the summer of 1972, we combined for three first places and three seconds in five weeks on the tour.

The Dick Weber Wrist Master is designed with a metal insert that makes it virtually impossible for your wrist to break as you release the ball. It also prevents wrist fatigue and helps stop sore thumbs by distributing the weight of the ball more evenly.

Don Carter has what is probably the most popular glove on the market. Don produced it himself when, during his heyday, he used to develop a large callus on his hand. Don's glove features a padded palm that keeps your ball in the same position at all times and causes less strain on your fingers and thumb. Because it covers most of the hand, it helps combat perspiration, much as does a golf glove, while providing a nonslip grip.

Billy Welu backs the Lift-Tru. It also has a metal insert, aimed primarily at keeping a bowler's wrist in the proper position throughout delivery and release.

Gripping Aids

There are many aids offered to help you grip the ball better—thumb and finger hole inserts made of cork, rubber, sandpaper, and many other things.

The most popular, I believe, is the Ace Mitchell Shur-Hook. These are small cork inserts that fit in the thumb or finger holes. They adhere by an adhesive backing and feature ridges to provide lift in addition to gripping qualities. Ace, now a bowling equipment store owner and a well-known bowling sponsor, estimates that sales of Shur-Hooks are now in the billions. Each year, 500,000 are exported to Japan alone.

FINGER IRRITATIONS

Finger and thumb irritations can occur whether you are a pro, bowling hundreds of games a week, or whether you are an advanced bowler. If you are a novice or intermediate, such ills usually occur because your ball doesn't fit properly or you are doing something wrong in your delivery. There are court plasters and clear plastic applicants you can use to shield against a sore thumb or fingers.

But before you try them, ask your pro, or another good bowler, to look you over in action. You may discover that the source of your discomfort is some part of your game that has gone astray or some part of your equipment that isn't fitted properly.

I can recall vividly an incident in 1967, when the PBA National Championship was the first bowling tournament ever staged in the new Madison Square Garden in New York. Dave Davis won the tournament. He won because he doctored up his ball during commercials on the nationally televised finals with small strips of tape inserted in the thumb hole of his ball to keep him from dropping it on his delivery. They were just strips of a national brand adhesive tape, not a marketed bowling aid.

I always carry some strips of black electrician's tape. I sometimes use a strip in the back of my thumb hole to enable me to get the thumb out more easily on release. If I'm dropping the ball or want to get it out farther over the *foul line*, I'll insert a strip to tighten the thumb hole.

This may give you a chuckle, but with the amount of bowling I do, I've found one of the best remedies for a sore thumb is a raw potato. That's right, I said raw potato! I got a lot of publicity out of the raw potato bit when I competed in the PBA U.S. Open at Madison Square Garden in 1972. Five of the top eight bowlers in the finals had sore thumbs.

I sent my wife out to buy a large raw potato, into which I cut a hole for my thumb. The starch did the job. After two hours of walking around with my thumb stuck in the potato, to everyone's smirks and kidding, my thumb felt as if I hadn't bowled in two weeks. I went on to win the tournament.

To sum up—forget aids until you have developed a good, solid game. Then, give them a try if you have some small fault you just can't seem to overcome. Aids have helped a lot of pros, so don't discount them as simply gimmicks. They could add a lot of pins to your score.

SCORING

At first, scoring in bowling may seem complicated and confusing. But you'll find scoring easy if you keep just two guidelines in mind:

1. A *spare* is scored when you knock down all the pins in two rolls. A spare is worth 10 points plus the number of pins knocked down on the next ball thrown.

2. A *strike* is scored when you knock down all the pins with your first ball. It, too, is worth 10 points, but you also count the number of pins toppled on the next *two* balls.

If you roll a spare, don't enter a score until after you have rolled the first ball of your next frame. If you have a strike, don't mark a score until you have rolled the next *two* balls.

On your first roll, you might bowl a *split*. A split occurs when you knock down the *head pin* and at least one other pin between two or more pins that are left standing. Or, you might knock down one or more pins that are immediately in front of pins that

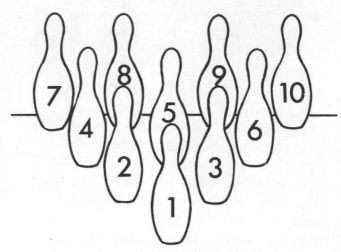

DIAGRAM 1. The bowling pins.

remain standing. As long as the head pin is down, either situation is a split.

Diagram 1 shows how the pins are numbered when they are set up. If you left only the 7 and 10 pins standing, you would have one of the most frustrating splits—one that is almost impossible to *convert*, or make into a spare.

There are some basic symbols that you must learn to use so that you will be able to look at your scoresheet for any given game and know exactly what you did to achieve your final score. These symbols are shown in Diagram 2.

On your scoresheet, each game is indicated by ten *frames*, or squares. In each frame, there is a smaller square in the upper righthand corner. The symbols go in these smaller squares. If you get a strike or a spare, put the symbol in the small box. If you get a split, enter a circle. If you convert the split, put the spare symbol through the split symbol—and congratulations! When

DIAGRAM 2. Symbols used in scoring.

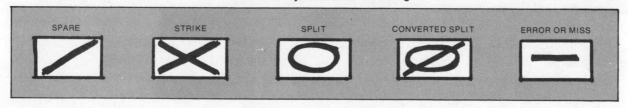

DIAGRAM 3. Scoring for a sample game.

you fail to strike, spare, or convert a split, you have erred. Put the error—or *miss*—symbol in the small box.

To make scoring clear to you, here's a shot-by-shot account of a game so that you can see how scoring symbols are used (Diagram 3).

Frame One. You knock down 7 pins on your first ball and the other 3 on your second. Mark the spare symbol in the small box, but don't mark in a score until your next ball.

Frame Two. Again you get 7 pins on the first roll. Now you've earned 10 points for the first-frame spare plus 7 points for the first ball of your second frame. Mark 17 in the first frame. On your second ball, you miss the remaining three pins. Mark an error, add 7 to your score, and enter 24 in the second frame.

Frame Three. Strike! Mark X in the small box, but don't put in a score until after your next two balls.

Frame Four. You knock over 8 on the first ball, and convert the other 2 on the second ball. You get 10 points for your third-frame strike plus 10 more for the fourth-frame spare—20 points on your strike. Mark 44 in the third frame. In the fourth frame, mark a spare but no score. Remember, you still have another ball to count toward the spare.

Frame Five. Strike! On top of your spare, this strike gives you 20 points. Your score is now 64 on the fourth frame, with your strike still working for you.

Frame Six. Strike! Hey, you're getting good. But don't mark any score yet in frames five and six.

Frame Seven. Tough luck. You knock down 8 pins but leave a split. You get 10 for each of your strikes in the fifth and sixth frames and add the 8 you've just knocked down. You'll therefore add 28 pins to your score of 64—mark 92 in the fifth frame. On your second ball, you convert the split. You get 10 for that plus 10 for your sixth-frame strike. These 20 points give you 112 in the sixth frame.

Frame Eight. Strike! That's 10 points plus 10 for your seventh-frame spare. That gives you 132 in the seventh frame, with a strike still working for you carrying over to the ninth.

Frame Nine. Another strike! Leave the eighth and ninth frames scoreless.

Frame Ten. Three strikes in a row! That's 30 points for strikes in frames eight, nine, and ten. Mark 162 in the eighth frame. Because your last ball was a strike, you now have two bonus balls to complete your strike score.

Bonus. Ugh! You get only 6 pins on the bonus ball. With your eighth and ninth frame strikes, this adds 26 to your score. Mark down 188 in the ninth frame. On your second bonus ball you make the spare. That's 10 pins plus 10 for your strike in the tenth frame. Add 20 to your score and enter it in the tenth frame. You've just bowled a 208 game.

As you can see by studying Diagram 3,

you get a high score in bowling by following up your spares and strikes with more of the same. If you fail to convert your spares, you miss that build-up of pins.

If you are bowling as part of a team, the scores of all your team members will be added together and matched against those of your opponents to determine the winner of a game. However, one of the teams may receive a handicap, which also will figure in the final score. Handicaps will be dealt with in detail in a later chapter on league bowling.

Learn how to score. It will make your game much more enjoyable if you can study your scoresheet afterward and know just where you went wrong—or what you did right.

DOs AND DON'Ts

DO buy your own ball as soon as possible. I recommend a plastic ball.

DON'T choose your ball without consulting the pro or the proprietor at your lanes, who can answer any questions you may have.

DO choose the heaviest ball you can con-

trol. A heavier ball will knock down more pins.

DON'T try to be a strongman or woman. If you find a lighter-weight ball that feels comfortable, buy it and don't feel self-conscious.

DO buy a conventional shoe.

DON'T be afraid to experiment with lowering or building up the heels of your shoes if your slide isn't what you want. A shoemaker can make inexpensive adjustments.

DO dress colorfully and stylishly. It may help your emotional attitude toward the game.

DON'T wear clothing that in any way restricts your bowling delivery.

DO ask your lane proprietor the weight and type of pins you are bowling against. It will help you to adjust your game to the type of wood—or plastic—you are facing.

DON'T feel that a bowling aid will make you an instant 200-average bowler. Develop a solid game first before experimenting with aids.

DO learn how to score. It makes the game more fun.

CONCENTRATION AND PRACTICE . . . are what develop good bowling. Go over every step until your technique is perfect. Here I'm showing Mary Ann the correct position for the thumb – between the 9 and 11 o'clock positions.

chapter 2
TECHNIQUE

How good a bowler you become is strictly up to you. If you work hard mastering the techniques that I am going to explain, I guarantee your scores will improve. We're going to start at the beginning for the novice bowler, but there will be tips for the intermediate and advanced bowler, too.

Practice and attention to detail are the keys to better bowling. I often bowl 100 practice games a week. Undoubtedly, you won't have that much time. But even if you bowl only once or twice a week, you can profit by what I'll be explaining in this and succeeding chapters—if you concentrate on trying to bowl correctly.

For the sake of clarity, my instructions are aimed at right-handed bowlers. If you are left-handed, simply reverse the instructions, unless I tell you otherwise.

GRIPS

There are three basic bowling grips: *conventional, semi-fingertip,* and *full-fingertip.*

I strongly recommend the conventional grip for all except advanced bowlers. The conventional grip, in which the thumb, middle finger, and ring finger are inserted into the ball, is the strongest grip for the average bowler. It will enable you to control the ball better.

In the conventional grip, your middle and ring fingers should be inserted in the ball first. They'll go in to about the second knuckle. Then insert your thumb.

Swing the ball back and forth a couple of times. It should feel snug but never tight on your fingers. You'll know right away whether you have control over the ball. If you feel as if you might drop the ball or you have to squeeze to control it, you should have your finger span or thumb hole checked by the lane pro. You can always have the holes plugged and new ones drilled.

As your game improves, you might want to try the semi- or full-fingertip grips, which are designed to increase the *hooking* characteristics of the ball. However, you'll

THE CONVENTIONAL GRIP.

THE FINGERTIP GRIP.

find these grips harder to control. Your grip will not be as strong as the conventional grip because your fingers won't be inserted as far into the ball.

The fingertip grips are achieved by widening the span between your thumb hole and the finger holes. For the semi-fingertip grip, your fingertips will be inserted in the ball only as far as between the first and second knuckles. On the full-fingertip grip, your fingers will go in only up to the first knuckles. Mastering the fingertip grips requires extensive practice. So if you are only an occasional bowler, stick with the conventional grip.

There are other grips, but none of them are advisable for the novice or intermediate bowler. Some bowlers use a two-finger grip—only the thumb and middle finger. Others use a "slot grip," one in which the two holes that accommodate the middle and ring fingers are joined to form a slot. The slot grip gives more consistent *lift* to the ball because the fingers may be positioned closer to each other in the slot.

Here's a grip that might help women bowlers. Two years ago, I experimented by drilling four holes, in addition to the thumb hole, in my ball. Thus I was able to place all my fingers in the ball. I called it my "claw grip." The grip really made the ball feel much lighter, and although I didn't stick with it, it might be ideal for a woman or a junior bowler who would like to throw a heavier ball but isn't strong enough to control one.

My mother-in-law uses the claw grip to throw a 16-pound ball. She says the grip makes the ball feel as if it weighs only 13 pounds. She's got a 150 average—and that's not bad for an older woman (she's 63) who has been bowling for only seven years.

FINGER POSITIONS

Next let's get your fingers positioned in the

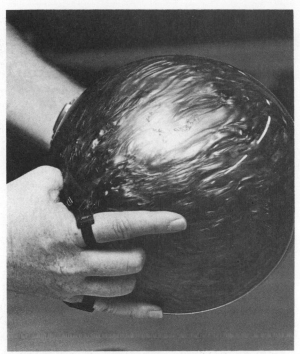

TEN O'CLOCK AND ALL'S WELL. If this position is maintained throughout delivery, the ball will lift and hook properly.

with the conventional grip. As you hold the ball in front of you ready to begin your delivery, your thumb should be in the 10 o'clock position. At the *point of release,* the 10 o'clock position will cause your hand to lift the ball from the side, which will give the ball a proper roll and *hook.*

A hook is a ball that curves as it rolls down the lane toward the pins. It is similar to a curve ball in baseball. The ball will curve from right to left for a right-handed bowler and from left to right for a left-handed bowler.

Many instructors like to start their novice bowlers out bowling a *straight ball* and then advance them to throwing a hook. But a ball that hooks is more desirable. Its curving action will cause the pins to mix and bounce off one another in a chain reaction —a reaction that is likely to cause a strike. As we progress, you'll see that it isn't that difficult to throw or control a hook.

If your thumb is in the 10 o'clock position at release, your hand and fingers will automatically give the lift and spin that will make the ball hook. You may find, however, that a 9 or 11 o'clock position makes the

ball so that you can come up with a perfect shot. There is no better way to illustrate correct finger positions than to refer to the face of a clock.

We'll assume you're holding the ball

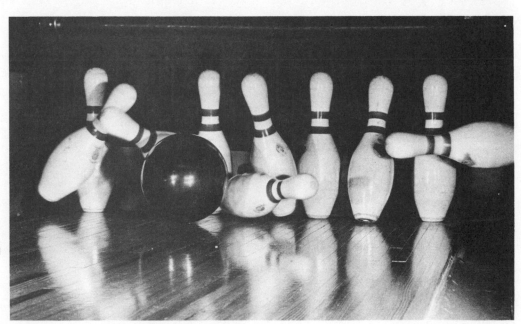

A HOOK BALL . . . produces this kind of mixing action, with the pins bouncing off each other in a chain reaction.

ball work better for you. But never let your thumb go higher or lower than those two checkpoints.

A "high noon" thumb position will most likely result in a straight ball or, worse yet, in a *backup ball*. A backup ball does just the opposite of what it's supposed to—it goes into the pins from left to right for a right-hander or from right to left for a left-hander.

If you let your thumb drop below the 9 o'clock mark you'll find that, upon delivery, you'll be overturning the ball and it will hook too quickly. The ball will strike the pins with no mixing action—a good way to come up with some dandy splits.

A final word about grips and finger positions: never squeeze the ball. When I am bowling well, I feel as if I'm holding a bird, not a 16-pound ball. Relax. Keep a firm wrist but don't squeeze. If you squeeze the ball, your thumb is likely to get caught in the ball and result in a poor shot—not to mention a sore thumb.

FOOTWORK

In any sport, footwork is very important. I don't believe the majority of bowlers attach enough importance to this phase of the game. Too many bowlers concentrate on the arm swing or the actual release of the ball, forgetting that without proper footwork they won't be able to accomplish either of those correctly.

The tendency seems to be to rush—to muscle the ball into motion and throw it as hard as possible. Actually, to become a good bowler, you must strive to do just the opposite.

Remember—bowling is walking. Taking it slow with the feet is vital. If you run up to the foul line you'll be off-balance 90 percent of the time, and your tempo will be destroyed.

Mike Durbin won the $125,000 Firestone Tournament of Champions using a three-step delivery. He used it because he is tall and has short arms. Dick Weber has experimented with a six-step delivery because he had some problems in getting the ball away at the proper instant. I use a five-step approach because it gives me a little more speed and helps me throw the ball a bit harder.

Obviously, the delivery you find most comfortable is the best. Years ago, Stan Gifford did quite well with an approach that included as many as eight short steps.

However, I think most bowlers will do best with a four-step delivery. Concentrate on developing slow feet, especially on your first two steps. I concentrate on the first two steps more than on the final two.

Here, broken down by steps, is what you must do (Diagram 4). Don't worry, for now, about your position on the lanes. I'll tell you how to set up and use vital targets and checkpoints in Chapter 3.

Starting Point

To find the proper spot on the *approach area* to start your delivery, place your heels about three inches from the foul line, facing away from the pins. Take four normal steps toward the rear of the approach and add a half step for the slide you'll take at the end of your delivery. Turn around and face the pins.

You should be standing somewhere near a row of dots located 12 feet from the foul line. There are three sets of these dots on the approach: one set at the foul line, one at the 12-foot mark, and one at the 15-foot mark, one foot from the rear of the approach.

Depending upon your height, stride and physical characteristics, you may have to adjust later if you find you are sliding over the foul line at the point of release or if you

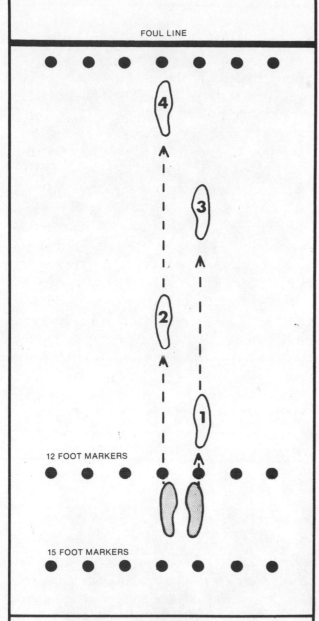

FOUL LINE

12 FOOT MARKERS

15 FOOT MARKERS

DIAGRAM 4. The four-step approach.

Face the pins squarely. Grip the ball with your right hand with the thumb in the 10 o'clock position. Place your left hand on the side or underneath the ball for support and balance. The ball should be held at or slightly below the waist.

Your first step should be short, perhaps only a half step. But you must get the ball in motion with it. As you step, push the ball out toward the pins about as far as the step itself. Don't rush. Make it natural.

Second and Third Steps

As soon as the first step is completed and the second begins, the left hand should come away from the ball. Let the weight of the ball make your right hand drop naturally. If the first two steps are made slowly and naturally, you will go automatically into your third step.

Personally, I don't concentrate on the third step because it is almost a reflex action if the first two steps are correct. The only thing you need remember is that on the third step the right leg must start to bend so that it will be in position for the fourth step and slide.

Fourth Step and Slide

At this point, you have built up the speed and arm swing necessary to roll the ball down the lane properly. Remember, I said *roll*. Never throw the ball. "Keep the ball rolling" is a good catch phrase to remember.

With your wrist still locked in the 10 o'clock thumb position, your right arm and left leg will move together. As the ball reaches the left foot on your downswing, you should have reached the end of the fourth step and slide, about three inches behind the foul line.

Your hand, however, will carry the ball over the foul line, where you release the ball. Your thumb must slip out of the ball

are reaching the end of your delivery a foot and a half short of the foul line. To adjust, start at the 4½-step location. Normally, you'll never get back as far as the 15-foot line unless you switch to a five-step delivery, take exceptionally long strides, or have an exaggerated slide.

First Step

In a four-step delivery, you'll begin with your right foot if you are right-handed.

APPROACH AND DELIVERY. Study this photo sequence carefully and notice the elements that are essential for a smooth delivery. I begin in a relaxed manner, with the ball held waist high. I push the ball out on my

backswing. On the fourth step, my left leg and right arm are moving together and my right leg is fully bent

first short step and let it fall naturally as I begin the second step. The third step is almost a reflex action — my shoulders are square and my arm is extended on the downswing, and my right leg starts to bend on the

for the slide. As I release the ball, my thumb leaves the ball just an instant before my fingers, which lift the ball over the foul line. My right foot keeps me in balance.

Notice that my arm keeps right on going for a smooth follow-through and a perfect delivery, every time.

first, an instant before the fingers. If your thumb was in proper position, the fingers will impart a slight lift and turn to the ball and produce a moderate hook.

Follow-Through

As in many other sports, the follow-through in bowling is extremely important. It gives you direction. If you can follow through properly, you did everything else in your delivery correctly.

I recommend a follow-through that is at least shoulder high. Reach out for your target and bring your arm up on a perpendicular plane that leads over your target. Extend your forearm so that your arm, as it swings up after releasing the ball, is held out almost straight, sweeping toward the ceiling. This will enable you to get the ball farther down the lane and give it the spin to make it hook at the desired point.

Study the photographs of my stance and footwork and then, within your own

physical limitations, try to imitate them. You don't have to go to the lanes to work on this all-important phase of the game. Simply go through the motions, with or without a ball, standing in front of a mirror where you can observe your form. The idea is to correlate the steps and swing, making them almost automatic. Develop a smooth tempo.

Remember that on your delivery bowling is walking. Haste will only make waste —your game will suffer.

SEVEN CHECKPOINTS

Down through the years I have developed a list of seven checkpoints to keep me in form on my approach. If I start bowling badly, they are the first things I check to see where my game has gone wrong.

I can't stress enough how important the approach and footwork are to your game. There is no way you can deliver a properly thrown strike or spare ball if you do not reach the point of release in perfect position.

You can do this only by developing a fluid approach in which every phase of the arm swing and footwork are synchronized. If something goes wrong with your delivery, my seven points should help solve your problems.

1. At the finishing position, where I release the ball, my sliding foot must be straight forward and pointed at the head pin. If my toe is pointed right of the head pin, I've made a bad shot. Somewhere, I've lost my tempo and timing and pulled myself off line.

2. My left leg must be fully bent for a smooth slide. The bending action must start with a bending of the right leg on the third step.

3. At the point of release my hips must be parallel to the foul line. I try to keep my right foot in contact with the floor, even after the left leg slide, to keep my hips square to target.

4. My shoulders must be parallel to the foul line at the point of release.

5. My follow-through must be at least shoulder high. There should be no swaying to the left or right with my body or with my arm swing.

6. My left arm, swinging free, must be used for balance. Even with a 16-pound ball pulling down on my right arm, the right shoulder must not collapse. The left arm should be carried waist high to counteract the pull of the ball on the right side of the body and to balance the overall shot.

7. My right foot, at least the toe, should be kept on the lane as much as possible. I drag the toe if necessary. This also adds to balance and a smooth delivery.

If your sliding foot stops while pointing to the left of the head pin when you slide and release the ball, don't fret. If your foot ends in this position, you have accomplished what pros call the *post position*. It's a good position, too, because it automatically means your shoulders are square to the pins at point of release. In other words you have come through well on your shot. Failing to complete a shot naturally causes the ball to slide sickeningly to the right of the desired target area. In golf, they call such a "revoltin' development" a slice.

Pro bowlers Mike Durbin, Barry Asher, and Norm Meyers all finish their deliveries in the post position. They have won a lot of money on the PBA tour because they do. A ball delivered in the post position will knock over a lot of pins because it will be a mixing ball, not one that slides weakly off target.

DOs AND DON'Ts

DO use a conventional grip.

DON'T try a semi- or full-fingertip grip until you feel confident that you are in complete control of your game.

DO position your thumb in a 10 o'clock position in the ball.

DON'T allow the thumb to be positioned on top of the ball or below the 9 o'clock level. If you do, you'll wind up with a backup or overturned ball.

DO spend time finding the proper distance from the foul line for your set-up and address positions.

DON'T rush your initial steps.

DO concentrate on a shoulder-high follow-through.

DO practice to achieve synchronized footwork and arm swing.

DO use my seven checkpoints if you find you are having trouble on approach and delivery.

AREA BOWLING . . . means shooting at the target arrows on the lane rather than at the pins. This ball will go across the second target arrow and hook into the strike pocket, exactly where I want it to go.

chapter 3
AREA BOWLING

It's time to start throwing strikes. We've covered all the basics—ball selection, shoes, grip, and footwork. Now let's start knocking down pins.

The secret to good bowling is what I call *area bowling*. The pros have other names for it, such as *spot bowling* or *target bowling*. I prefer to call it area bowling because that's what you will be shooting at —various areas on the lane, not any one absolute spot or target.

Before I explain how I use these areas, there are a few things you should know about the lane itself (Diagram 5). I would guess that most bowlers, even beginners, know that the distance from the foul line to the head pin is 60 feet. A few may also know that the distance from the foul line to the *pit end* is 63 feet and 3/16 inch.

However, you can ask even intermediate bowlers the width of a lane or how many boards go into its construction and be answered by a blank stare. That's why they are only intermediate bowlers. To be a good bowler, you must know these figures and use them as vital aids to your game.

Lanes are 41 to 42 inches wide and are composed of 39 boards. Boards are strips of wood approximately 1 and 1/16 inches wide that are laid side by side to form the surface on which you bowl. The boards and the dots and arrows on the lane serve as guidelines and checkpoints to better bowling. You must understand how to use them to improve your game.

DOTS AND ARROWS

There are three sets of dots on the approaches to the bowling area of the lane. The dots are located at the foul line and 12 and 15 feet back from the foul line.

Usually each set consists of seven dots. These dots are aligned with each other and also with a set of seven triangular-shaped target arrows that start 10 to 15 feet down the lane. In some lanes, however, there are only five dots to a set, with no dots lined up

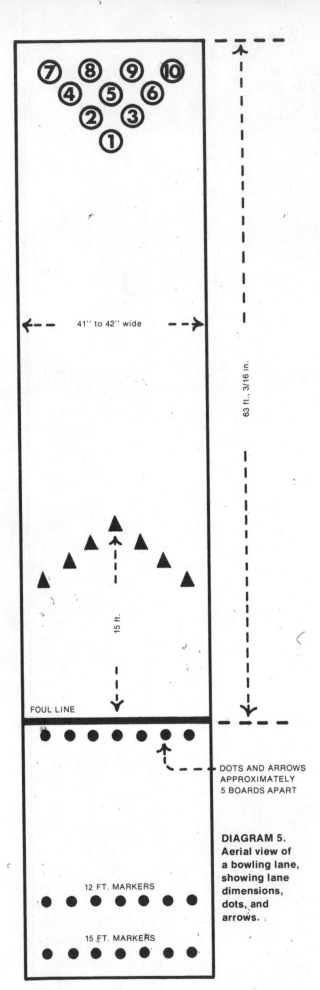

41'' to 42'' wide

63 ft., 3/16 in.

15 ft.

FOUL LINE

— DOTS AND ARROWS
APPROXIMATELY
5 BOARDS APART

DIAGRAM 5.
Aerial view of
a bowling lane,
showing lane
dimensions,
dots, and
arrows.

12 FT. MARKERS

15 FT. MARKERS

THE DOTS ON THE LANE . . . aren't there just for
decoration. They're to help you align your ball and
adjust your delivery.

with the first target arrows on the right and left.

Each dot and arrow is spaced five boards from the next. Thus the first dot on the approach and the first arrow down lane are five boards from the righthand edge of the lane. The second dot and arrow are 10 boards from the right edge of the lane, and so on.

SETUP

In the preceding chapter I told you how to determine how far from the foul line you should be for your approach. Now let's set you up at the most advantageous spot in that area.

I suggest that you concentrate on the second target arrow down lane as a guide

THE SECOND TARGET ARROW . . . is ten boards from the right channel. This is your target for all strike shots.

while you are mastering area bowling. That arrow will be the one 10 boards from the right edge of the lane. It is the most heavily traveled area on most bowling lanes. Your goal will be to roll the ball over the second arrow on the first ball of every frame. You must start your approach from a place that will enable you to do this. Here's where the dots on the approach will serve you well.

Let's assume you are just learning to bowl. You probably will have only a small hook, for it takes time and practice to develop the proper spin and number of revolutions needed for the most desired shot. At first, your ball most probably will angle into the pins instead of hooking into them. But don't despair. The area bowling concept can guide you through this frustrating stage.

In order to get your ball out and over the second target arrow on a proper line to the *strike pocket*, between the 1- and 3-pins, you must set up at the proper spot on the approach. For a left-handed bowler, the

strike pocket is between the 1- and 2-pins (Diagram 6). If you're an average bowler, you'll probably find that when you release the ball it will hit the lane at a spot about seven boards to the right of where your left foot slides to a stop. With that in

DIAGRAM 6. The 1-2 pocket, your strike target if you are left-handed.

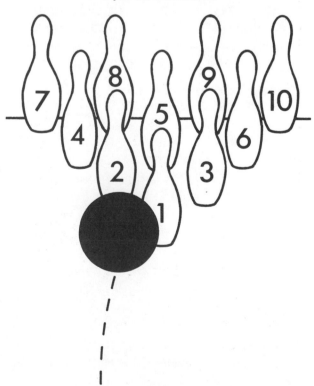

MY LEFT FOOT . . . is at the center dot both when I start and at the point of release. Because your hook won't be exactly the same as mine, you won't necessarily begin at the same place, but your left foot should slide down the same board on which you started.

mind, here's how you should set up to throw a small hook or angling shot in the proper manner. Later you may have to make adjustments for such factors as height and stride.

Position your left toe or the instep of your left foot in line with the 15th board, or the third dot, on the approach. Place your right foot close to the left for balance and weight distribution. Make sure your right foot is in a comfortable position.

Look down lane at the pins—but only briefly. Just make sure all pins are standing and that no pins from the previous rack have been missed by the pinspotter.

Now forget about the pins. Forget they are even down there. Switch your gaze to the second target arrow (Diagram 7). Don't look at the pins again until you are well into your follow-through at the end of your shot. This is a vital point.

It is much easier to hit the second arrow, 15 to 20 feet down lane, than it is to hit the head pin and strike pocket 60 feet away. If you hit the target arrow with a properly delivered ball, you have an excellent chance of slamming into that strike pocket, which seems so far away. Besides, zeroing in on a small arrow relatively close to you will help you concentrate more on your delivery than on watching the pins to see which ones will fall.

THE DELIVERY

You're set up with your left foot at the 15th board. Face the pins squarely, with your eyes fixed on the second target arrow. Go into your approach, keeping your feet slow. Move straight forward without turning or twisting your body.

At the point of release, your left foot must slide right down the 15th board on

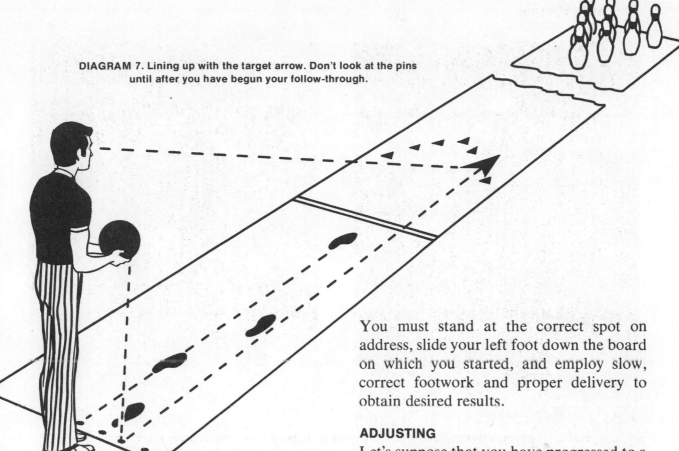

DIAGRAM 7. Lining up with the target arrow. Don't look at the pins until after you have begun your follow-through.

You must stand at the correct spot on address, slide your left foot down the board on which you started, and employ slow, correct footwork and proper delivery to obtain desired results.

ADJUSTING

Let's suppose that you have progressed to a point where you are throwing a medium rather than a small hook. You must adjust. Should you move your target area or your feet? I think you should move your feet.

To compensate for your larger hook, move your left foot from the 15th board to the 19th board, one board to the right of the center approach dot. Deliver your ball as before. But you will no longer slide down the board on which you started. This time you must walk *toward the target arrow* instead of straight forward. The drift of your feet will allow you to *lay out* the ball on the 11th or 12th board. It will roll from there across the second arrow and then hook back into the strike pocket.

If you graduate to a big hook, follow the same procedure. Move four more boards to the left and position your left foot on the 23rd board, three boards to the left of the center dot. At the point of release, your

which you started. This will allow the ball to be lifted across seven boards and roll over the eighth board as it comes down on the lane. With a small hook or angling action, the ball will cross the second target arrow (10th board) and proceed into the strike pocket.

I'm using the figure of seven boards because that is about average. But you may discover that the range between where your left foot stops and where your ball hits the lane is wider than seven boards. I think, though, that if your range is more than eight boards your arm swing is out of kilter and needs attention. If your span is less than six boards, you had better buy shin guards, because you are going to be hitting your left ankle when you release the ball.

As you can see, the movements that you have learned up to this point must be synchronized if the area system is to work.

ball will land on the 14th or 15th board. It will swing out to cross the second arrow and then hook back into the strike pocket.

As your hook increases, the key is that you must always walk toward your target arrow. If you throw a straight ball or a slight hook, your target is straight in front of you and you can approach it head on. As your hook gets bigger, you'll be walking at a greater and greater angle toward the target arrow.

The amount you need to adjust will depend, of course, on the size of your hook. You'll have to experiment to find exactly the right spot for you.

Perhaps you're doing everything just as I have instructed, but your ball still isn't hitting the strike pocket. Again, I think you should adjust your feet, not your target area. Let's say you threw the ball properly over the target area, but your ball went to the right of the head pin and strike pocket. To adjust, move your feet to the *right*. Try moving over two boards. Shoot again, and observe the results (See Diagram 8).

Suppose that this time the ball hits the head pin on the nose. You overadjusted. Move back one board to the left and try again. If your ball is crossing over to the left side of the pins and striking what is called the *Brooklyn* (1-2 pocket), you should adjust to the left in the same manner. Adjust a board or two at a time until you're once again throwing to the right side of the rack. Remember, you're still using the second target arrow.

Imagine a large board swinging on a pivot. If you moved one end of the board to the left, the other end would move to the right. That is the principle on which adjustment works. The target arrow is the pivot point of the board. If you want your ball to go to the left, you must move your feet to the right; if you want the ball to go to the right, move your feet to the left.

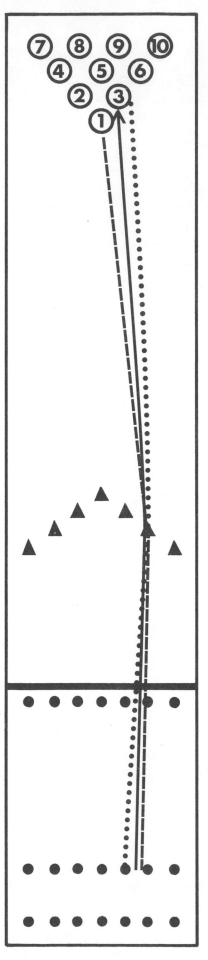

**DIAGRAM 8.
Adjusting your
shot.**

SPEED

Many bowlers feel that they must over-power the pins to knock them down. This is untrue, especially with today's bouncy, plastic-coated pins. Under today's lane conditions, a medium or slow ball will carry more pins. Anyone who throws a cannonball risks getting powder burns. The super-speed thrower will often leave the 4-pin, the third pin back from the head pin on the left. What happens is that the 2-pin, which is supposed to bounce back and topple the 4, will, on a strong ball, be sent sailing straight off the side wall, missing the 4-pin completely.

Did you ever consider that on a perfect strike shot only four pins—the 1-, 3-, 5-, and 9 pins   will come in contact with the ball? The rest of the pins are knocked down by chain reaction, triggered by speed, the revolution of the ball, and the angle of attack (Diagram 9). You must throw a ball that is slow enough to give all the pins a chance to do their intended jobs.

A good example of the change in think-ing on speed since 20 years ago is Dick Hoover, a past PBA star, now a lanes owner in Ohio. Hoover threw what was probably the fastest and hardest ball in pro history. Against the old, heavy, wood pins, his ball worked miracles. Against modern, flying, plastic-coated pins, however, such a ball creates many splits and one-pin *leaves*. I've got to think that the emergence of the plastic pin hastened Dick's retirement. He was one of the greatest pocketshooters who ever lived, but his powerhouse ball just wouldn't carry today's bouncy pins.

Most of the good, young pros coming on tour today have developed medium or very slow deliveries. One who has super-slow speed is Tommy Hudson. A rookie in 1972, he made the finals in four of the first six events he entered. The key to his game is his slow delivery. The ball knocks those 4-

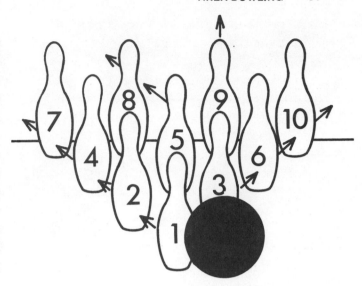

DIAGRAM 9. The action of the pins on a strike.

pins over beautifully. He gets a lot of mix-ing action and often can carry the rack for a strike even though he doesn't get a solid pocket hit.

So far, we've talked about the area method of bowling in relation to the first, or strike, ball. In the next chapter, we'll find that the method has even more value for converting spares.

DOs AND DON'Ts

DO study the dimensions of the lane and its dots and arrows. They are the keys to area bowling.

DO use the second target area as a guide for mastering the area concept for strikes.

DO position your left foot seven boards left of where you will want to have your ball land on the lane.

DO reach point of release with your shoulders and body square to the pins.

DON'T move your target on adjust-ments. Move your feet.

DON'T watch the pins during your delivery. Concentrate on your target arrow.

DON'T throw the ball hard. A medium or slow speed will knock over more pins.

A WIDE-OPEN SPLIT . . . is the frustration of every bowler. Some splits are practically impossible to convert, but most of them can be mastered by using my area bowling technique.

chapter 4
SHOOTING SPARES

In 1971, Larry Laub and I each rolled a 237 game to tie for the championship in the Brunswick World Open. Following the format of the televised PBA tour, we engaged in a two-frame rolloff to determine the winner.

There is no room for mistakes in a two-frame rolloff. However, I made a mistake in the first frame and left a 6-7-10-pin split. I would estimate my chances of picking up that split at 200 to 1 because of the big hook I throw. But I had no choice. I had to try to convert it. If it had been earlier in the game, I'd have gone for two pins, the 6 and 10, playing it safe. Now it was do or die.

Well, I made the split for a spare and eventually won the two-frame rolloff 39 to 38. It was the greatest spare—and split—I've ever made. Not only did it give me a $12,000 check but it also gave me my sixth PBA win of the year. Johnny Petraglia had five tournament wins and several thousand dollars more in tour winnings, but I was elected Bowler of the Year. I'm sure that

victory influenced the voters in my favor.

This incident demonstrates the importance of spare shooting in bowling. The object of the game, of course, is to throw strikes. But as in any sport, no player is a machine. You can't make a hole-in-one in golf or hit a home run in baseball every time. You must settle for something less— but you can't disregard lesser accomplishments if you hope to become a top performer.

In the course of your bowling career, you'll shoot many more spares than you will strikes. Spares demand as much concentration as the strike shot. You must learn a myriad of moves on the lanes because of the variety and clusters of pins that can be left after you roll an unsuccessful strike shot. You need hours of practice to master spare shooting, but those hours of practice can make an average bowler an outstanding one.

Consider that you need only make two strikes in succession and convert all your spares in order to score a 200 game, the goal of every bowler. If you can alternate strikes and spares in any game, you'll have a perfect 200. We call it a *Dutch 200.*

Matches are often decided on the ability to make just one pin, not the whole rack. In 1963, Billy Hardwick needed to make only the 10-pin on the final frame to win the PBA Portland Open. For some reason, probably lack of concentration, Billy threw the ball into the channel. He lost first place to Darylee Cox because of this error.

The big difference between bowlers is strikes and spares. I think there are three categories of bowlers. The beginner is not proficient at making either strikes or spares and struggles to make a 150 average. The intermediate bowler makes his spares and his average climbs to 170. A good bowler, with an average of up to 190 or over, is the one with ability to string strikes.

The pros figure they must make 95 percent of their spare shots, allowing for unconvertible splits, if they are to make a good living. If you are to roll good scores, you must become proficient enough to make 80 percent of the spares with which you'll be confronted. Extending my area bowling concept will help you to attain this goal. But first, a few words on why spares occur when you just *know* you've thrown a perfect strike ball.

PERFECTION—AND DEFLECTION

You've just buried your strike shot in the 1-3 pocket (1-2 if you are left-handed) and shockingly, there stands a 10-pin, a 4-pin, or a split. What went wrong?

Most likely, the problem is the deflection of your ball off the pins, magnified by the speed with which you delivered the ball and today's bouncy, plastic-coated pins. As I told you in the previous chapter, a strike ball probably will strike no more than four pins—1, 3, 5, and 9. The rest of the strike

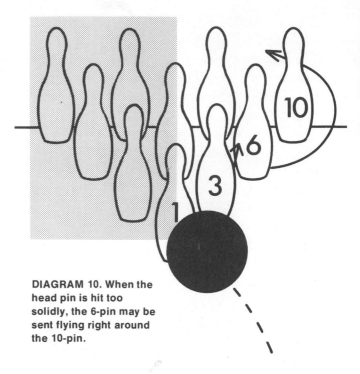

DIAGRAM 10. When the head pin is hit too solidly, the 6-pin may be sent flying right around the 10-pin.

shot is accomplished by the pins' mixing action. If your ball hooks too early and has no spin or hook left when it reaches the strike pocket, it likely will deflect to the right. The resulting pin action will not be sufficient to carry the rack of 10 pins. You'll end up with a lot of 10-pin leaves. In bowling parlance, we call this *getting tapped.* When it reaches the strike pocket, a ball with too little "oomph" on it will strike the head pin lightly, deflect into the 3-pin, and send the 3-pin straight back instead of to the right. The 6-pin will be struck a glancing blow by the 3-pin, pop straight out into the channel, and fail to knock down the 10-pin.

If you come into the pocket too strongly, the opposite will happen. The head pin will be struck too solidly. The 3-pin will get only a glancing blow on the left by your ball and will sail out, possibly missing both the 6- and 10-pins (Diagram 10).

It seems impossible, but the 5-pin, right smack in the middle of all that explosive action, will sometimes refuse to fall. Again, it's a matter of deflection. You've thrown a very weak ball, one with few revolutions. It has hit the pocket with nothing on it. The ball slides right, failing to drive into the 5-pin.

How about the 4-9, a common split? You are probably rolling a very strong ball. You hit the head pin too strongly. The 2-pin, which should kick out the 4, is kicked left by impact and goes around its intended victim. The 9-pin stands because your ball was driving so strongly that it went to the left of the 9-pin, with no deflection.

If you come up short of the strike pocket, nicking the head pin and striking the 3-pin too solidly, you may well get the 1-2-4-10 split, what we call the *washout*. Again, the 3-pin, struck too solidly, goes straight back, tips the 6-pin on the inside, and glances the 6-pin into the channel, missing the 10-pin.

If you have thrown what seems to be a perfect strike ball and you still have some pins standing, your problem could be the angle at which you are playing, the speed of your ball, or the weight of the pins. The pins nowadays are so bouncy that, even when struck perfectly, they might bounce right over the top of the pins they should have taken out.

You must accept these frustrations and concentrate on converting spares. Work hard to make every first ball a strike. But don't despair if a pesky pin or two fails to go down. It can happen to anyone. My biggest thrill in bowling occurred in 1970 when I won the Firestone Tournament of Champions in Akron. In the championship game, with the national TV audience watching, I rolled 11 straight strikes. I had already won the championship and its $25,000 first prize. But if I could throw one more strike for a perfect 300 game, I'd get a $10,000 bonus plus a new car.

I thought I threw my best strike ball of the game on that 12th roll. I was just sure it was a strike. In the tension, I dropped flat on the floor and covered my eyes with my hands. I heard a roar, and then a groan, from the packed house. When I peeked out, there was the 10-pin standing defiantly. No perfect game, no $10,000, no new car—and on a perfect hit, no less!

I've watched films of that last throw a hundred times, trying to discover just what went wrong. I believe that, because I was charged up, I threw that last ball just a little too hard. Pow! The deflection of the pins was altered. The 6-pin just flew right around the 10 and failed to kick it out.

But then, statistics compiled in 1971-72 on bowlers who had 299 games showed that the 10-pin was usually the pin that stopped their 300 bids. You must take these breaks in stride and carry on. In succeeding pages, I'm going to show you how to turn such despair into happiness.

Here's a tip that might help you discover why you aren't getting a strike—why all those pins are standing on what seem to be good hits.

If you toss a couple of balls that look as if they should be strikes but don't end up that way, quit watching the pins as they fly and focus on your ball. Watch where it goes, how it reacts, and where it drops off the lane at the end of your shot.

The ball should strike the 1-, 3-, 5-, and 9-pins. On a solid pocket hit, the 5-pin should take out the 8-pin. However, the manner in which the 5 takes the 8 is important. Watch where the ball drops off the lane. If it drops off in an area between where the 5- and 9-pins stood, good—you've got a driving ball. But if it drops off where the 9 stood, your ball is deflecting too much and eventually will get you in trouble if you don't adjust your speed, angle, or delivery.

SINGLE-PIN SPARES
Single-pin spares are the easiest to convert

I FELL FLAT ON MY FACE . . . so I wouldn't have to watch the crucial final ball in the championship match of the 1970 Firestone Tournament of Champions. A strike would have meant a 300 game, a new car, and $10,000. Even Dick Ritger, whom I had already defeated for the championship, was rooting for me. But the stubborn 10-pin defied me, and I had to settle for 299.

THE PIN THAT DIDN'T FALL . . . is my souvenir of the most frustrating moment in my pro career. I did win the championship, though — Mary Ann is holding my first-place prize money, a check for $25,000.

for some bowlers and the most difficult to make for others. The problem is chiefly psychological. If you're a novice you may have trouble with single pin spares because you have not yet developed confidence and accuracy. You'd much rather shoot at a multiple-pin spare on which you might get unexpected help from some of the other pins.

If you're an intermediate or advanced bowler, you have developed enough accuracy to take single-pin spares in stride. But you may now fear the multiple-pin shots because you know that, while you might get a lucky kick, the majority of the time you must deliver a ball at the exact angle and position necessary to convert all the pins.

For purposes of instruction, we'll use the

righthanded approach to single-pin pickups. If you are left-handed, just reverse the process.

Let's talk first about what I call the "left-handed spares." These are spares that involve pins on the left side of the lane, the 2-, 4-, 7-, and 8-pins. Here is where area bowling really comes into play. In shooting left-handed spares, never alter your target, the arrow down-lane over which you will bowl. However, you will move your feet to obtain a proper angle.

How far to the right you will move your feet will depend upon whether you throw a straight ball, a medium hook, or a big hook. You must determine the size of your own hook through practice and game conditions. But as a guide, I suggest you try a three-board adjustment on your spare shots.

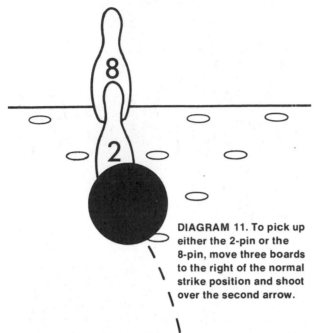

DIAGRAM 11. To pick up either the 2-pin or the 8-pin, move three boards to the right of the normal strike position and shoot over the second arrow.

Move your feet three additional boards from your starting point on the strike position for each pin you attempt to convert.

For instructional purposes, we will assume you are throwing a medium hook. As I suggested in Chapter 3, you will line up your left foot on the 19th board and use the second arrow as a target for the strike shot. You will then move your feet, seldom your target, from this position to make your spare shots.

It won't happen often, but let's start at the top and say that you leave the head pin. You may need no adjustment at all on your spare shot. However, just to make sure, I suggest you move one board to the right, to the 18th board, and try your strike shot again.

Suppose you've left the 2-pin. Move three more boards to the right, to the 15th board, and convert by throwing over the second arrow. You can convert the 8-pin in a similar fashion, since the 8 is located directly behind the 2 (Diagram 11). To pick up the 4-pin, move another three boards to the right, to the 12th board, and hit that second arrow again.

Let's say you've left the 7-pin. Again, move three additional boards to the right, to the 9th board, and stick with that second target arrow. It's as simple as that. As you can see, the farther to the left the pin is standing, the farther to the right you will move.

Where does this "left-handed spare" thinking leave the 5-pin? You shoot the 5 just as you would the 1 since it is one of the four pins your ball should strike on a perfect strike shot.

Now let's talk about the right-handed spares. These are pins on the right side of the lane, the 3-, 6-, 9-, and 10-pins.

For right-handed spares, however, you will also need to change your target arrow for a better angle of attack, since now you will be shooting *across* the lane instead of angling in with your natural hook. I'll show you how to make this major adjustment on your first move: after that, the three-board adjustment will prevail.

To make the 3- or 9-pin, move 10 boards to the left of your normal strike position while also moving your target from the second to the third arrow down-lane. If you have a medium hook, this would position your left foot on the 29th board. Your target will be the 15th board (third arrow).

To pick up the 6-pin, move your feet 13 boards to the left of strike position. Again shoot for the third arrow.

Now there stands the 10-pin, the most difficult pin for any right-handed bowler to convert because of the angle at which you must bowl and the pin's proximity to the channel. Exercise extreme caution—picking up this pin allows less margin for error than any other. You just can't take the chance of throwing the ball off the lane or of flinching and missing on the inside because of fear of the channel.

If you throw a medium hook, move your feet 16 boards to the left of strike position

PICKING UP THE 7-PIN . . . is easy if you're right-handed, but it's the most difficult single-pin spare for a left-handed bowler. Since the pin is on the far left, I begin my approach on the far right, with my left foot on the ninth board.

THE 10-PIN . . . is the hardest pin for a right-handed person to pick up, although a left-handed bowler can convert it easily. I begin my approach as far to the left as possible, to allow for my big hook. On this shot, your target should be the third arrow.

and shoot at the third arrow. If the 19th board is your strike position, this places your left foot at the 35th board; your angle of approach is toward the 15th board, the third arrow.

Right about now you are saying, "Whoa! Didn't you tell me always to start and finish on the same board on which I set up? How can I start and finish on the 35th board and ever hope to roll the ball across the 15th board, if I don't have arms like Gargantua?"

You are shooting cross-alley on right-handed spares, and you must allow for drift of your feet. On these shots, you no longer walk in a straight line down the starting board. Instead, walk *toward the target*, the arrow down-lane you are using as a checkpoint.

As you walk towards the arrow, your feet will probably drift seven boards. Your left foot will slide at release on the 28th board. You will lay the ball down seven more boards to the right on the 21st board, and it will cross over the 15th board area on its way to knocking over that pesky 10-pin.

If you tried to start and finish on the 35th board, you'd have to loop your arm out of proper swing to even attempt to reach the third arrow. You probably couldn't do it, no matter how you tried. That's why I emphasize walking *toward* your target and letting the drift of your feet and your natural, unrestricted swing automatically take care of the rest. At the point of release, your feet still will be parallel to your target as they should be.

Because it is so difficult to convert the 10-pin, however, I would suggest that anyone who throws a medium or big hook overadjust to be on the safe side.

I throw a big hook. In order to get the 10-pin, my adjustment is to move my feet all the way to the 45th board and switch my target to the fourth arrow. "But," you

protest, "the lanes are only 42 inches wide!" The approaches, however, are wider. I actually line up for the 10-pin standing in line with the channel on the left-hand side of the approach. I walk toward my target, the 20th board. My foot will slide at point of release on about the 38th board. I'll lay the ball out at approximately the 31st board, and the ball will roll out across the 20th board target on its way to the 10-pin. If the seven-board variation seems to differ at the end of my approach, please remember that I throw a very large hook and am able to compensate for it with a wrist turn that only a professional should attempt.

A lot of pros who throw a big hook are bothered by long ball-returning equipment, which prohibits the extreme left position I play for the 10-pin pickup. I've missed a lot of 10-pins on lanes where I must start at the 42nd board instead of the 45th because of the length of the ball return. With a lesser angle and my big hook, I wind up missing the 10 on the inside.

The 10-pin is the most difficult one-pin pickup for any right-handed bowler, just as the 7-pin is for a left-hander. The 10-pin sits on the fifth board, five boards in from the channel on the right side of the lane. Your bowling ball is roughly 8½ inches wide. If you throw the ball down the outside, you've got about two inches of space on the right side of the lane. If you miss by an inch, your ball will topple into the gutter.

Why isn't the 7-pin as difficult? For a left-handed bowler, it is. But a right-hander has the whole lane upon which to hook the ball in and sweep or clip off the 7-pin.

THE CLUSTERS

Here you will be shooting at a group of pins that has been left by your errant strike shot. In picking up these spares, go for the

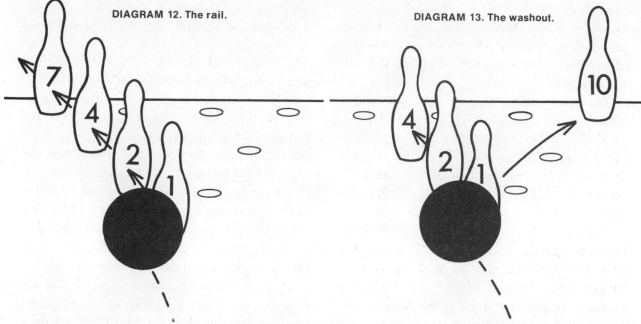

DIAGRAM 12. The rail.

DIAGRAM 13. The washout.

key pin, the pin closest to you in the cluster.

Of course, the ball must strike each of these clusters at a certain angle for a successful conversion. Study the accompanying diagrams for the proper angles.

I think it is even more important, however, to get your feet and target area in position to deliver the ball to its proper point of impact. Here then, is how I suggest you shoot the clusters, remembering that all board adjustments are from your normal strike position.

1-2, 1-2-4, and 1-2-4-7. To make *the rail,* move three boards to the right of your strike position. Shoot for the second target arrow. (Diagram 12.)

1-2-4-10. This spare is called the washout. You can make it with very little trouble by moving four boards to the right of your strike position. Again, aim for that second target arrow. Your goal is to hit the 2-pin. Just forget that the   4- and 10-pins exist. If you hit the 2-pin properly, you'll have an excellent chance of converting all four pins. (Diagram 13.)

1-3. Roll your normal strike ball.

1-5. Move one board to the right; shoot at the second arrow.

2-4. Move five boards to the right; use the second arrow for your target.

2-5. Move three boards to the right; shoot at the second arrow.

4-7. Move eight boards to the right of your strike position and aim for the second target arrow. (Diagram 14.)

3-5. Roll your normal strike ball.

3-6. Adjust for this spare by moving 11 boards left of your strike position. Shoot

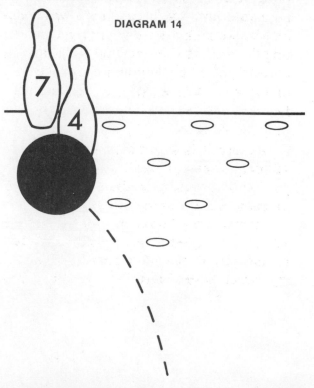

DIAGRAM 14

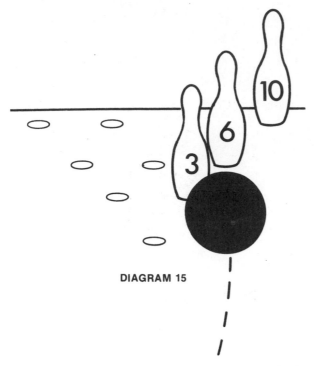

DIAGRAM 15

over the third target arrow. (Diagram 15.)

6-10. You'll convert this spare easily by moving 14 boards to the left and aiming for the third arrow. (Diagram 16.)

Remember: On all right-hand clusters, walk *toward* your target and lay the ball out so that it will roll over your target. At the point of release, reach for the target arrow to keep your ball in line.

Don't get too wrapped up in trying to hit the key pin on this side or that. Just hit the pin with a well-delivered ball from the start-

DIAGRAM 16

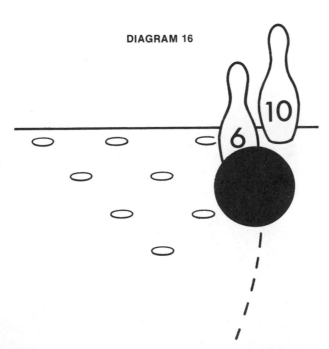

ing positions and target areas I suggest and you'll make the spares more times than you'll miss.

SPLITS AND TOUGHIES

Splits are the frustration of any bowler. It always seems that, just when you've got everything going for you, there stands a split to ruin your score. Because there are pins missing between those that are left standing, the degree of difficulty in converting is increased.

Sometimes a leave that is not classified as a split can be vexing. I call these leaves "toughies." Don't be defeated by a split or a toughie. They are not easy to convert, but only four, the 4-6, 7-10, 8-10, and 7-9, are considered virtually impossible to make.

Even those splits sometimes can be converted, if you are lucky. But the best advice on those four combinations is to go for one of the pins and be happy if you make it. Once, in a major tournament, Billy Welu was faced with the 7-10 split. This split is lovingly referred to by the pros as *mule ears, fenceposts, goalposts, bedposts, telephone poles*, and an assortment of less printable nicknames.

Billy correctly decided to play it safe and went for one pin, the 7. But that pin hit the *kickback*, rebounded out of the pit, and knocked down the 10. So nothing is really impossible in bowling. But the general rule is: on a seemingly impossible conversion, play it safe unless a conversion can mean victory or a super game. Then speed up your spare shot and hope for a lucky kick by one pin out of the pit.

What's the toughest spare for me? Without doubt, it's the 2-4-5 or the 2-4-5-8, the split we call the *bucket*. It's tough for anyone who throws a big hook as I do. The tendency is to hit the head pin thinly, leaving this spare. I think a survey of the PBA pros would find that this is the most

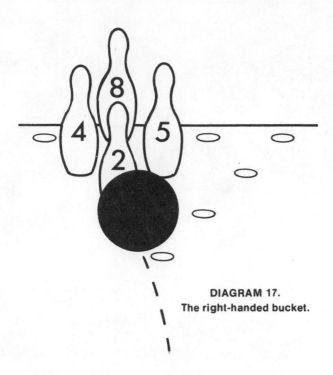

DIAGRAM 17.
The right-handed bucket.

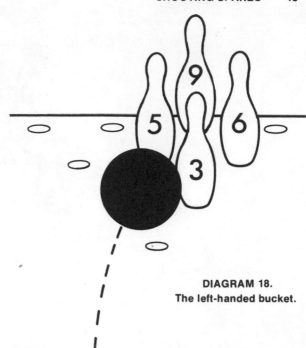

DIAGRAM 18.
The left-handed bucket.

difficult spare to pick up. My problem is that with my big hook I'm liable to chop the 2-4-8 with my spare shot and leave the 5-pin laughing at me.

The way to make the bucket is to move three boards to the right of your strike position and to aim for the second target arrow. (Diagram 17.)

For a left-handed bowler, the 3-5-6-9 is the bucket spare. To make this spare, reverse the procedure for right-handers. (Diagram 18.)

I think most pros would agree that the 3-6 or the 3-6-10 are the second most difficult spares in the game, because you are shooting cross-alley and can chop the 3 off the 6 or the 3-6 off the 10.

Again, we're using the area bowling concept to master the most common splits and toughies. We've already handled one of the most common toughies—the washout. Making such spares as these can give you just as much of a kick as making strikes, even though it won't add as many points to your score.

Next let's deal with the 2-7 and the 3-10,

what we call the *baby* splits. On the 2-7 split, shoot as if you were trying to hit the 4-pin, which normally stands between the 2- and 7-pins. Move seven boards to the right, shoot toward the second arrow, and fit your ball into the spot where the 4-pin normally stands. (Diagram 19.)

It's just the opposite on the 3-10 split. On this split, you'll shoot for the spot where the 6-pin should be. Move 13 boards to the left, shoot at the third target arrow, and fit the ball between the two pins. (Diagram 20.)

DIAGRAM 19

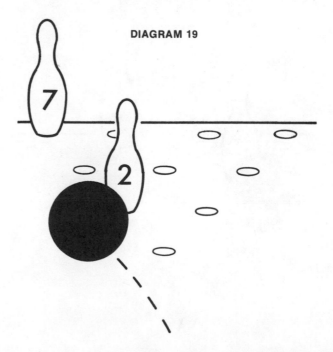

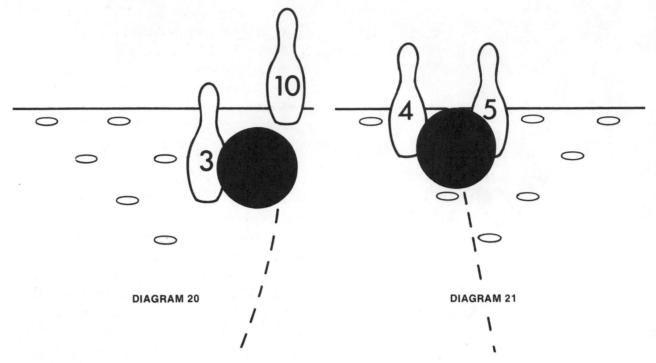

DIAGRAM 20

DIAGRAM 21

Here are my suggested adjustments for other common splits and tough leaves. For all adjustments, start at your normal strike position.

4-5, 2-4-5, 2-4-5-8. Move four boards to the right; shoot at the second arrow. (Diagram 21.)

4-9. Shoot as you would to hit the 7-pin. Adjust ten boards to the right; shoot at the second arrow. Also use this position for other 4-pin-oriented spares: 4-7-10, 4-7-9-10, or 4-10.(Diagram 22.)

5-10, 5-8-10. Move four boards to the right; aim at the second arrow. (Diagram 23.)

5-7. Move three boards to the left; shoot for the second arrow. (Diagram 24.)

Another kind of split is the *nose split*. Nose splits are caused by striking the head pin head on, or hitting it too solidly.

6-7, 6-7-10, 6-7-9-10. Shoot as if you were making the 10-pin pickup. Move feet 16 boards to the left; switch from the second to the third target arrow. If you throw

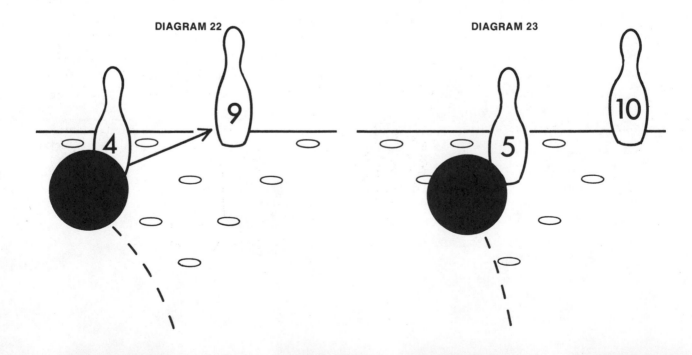

DIAGRAM 22

DIAGRAM 23

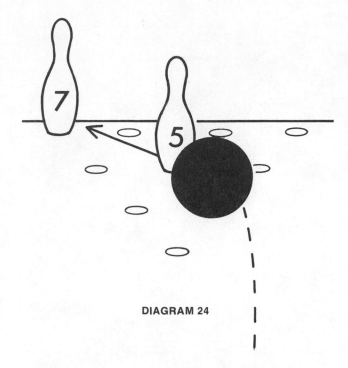

DIAGRAM 24

a big hook, try moving 23 boards to the left and using the fourth arrow. (Diagram 25.)

7-8. Shoot as you would the 4-pin. Move seven boards to the right; aim for the second arrow.

9-10. Shoot as you would for the 6-pin; move 13 boards to the left; use the third arrow.

3-6-7-10. Move 13 boards to the left; aim for the third arrow. Concentrate on hitting the 6-pin.

If you get one of the four impossible

DIAGRAM 25

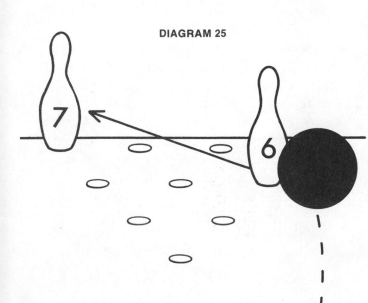

splits I mentioned, 4-6, 7-10, 8-10, 7-9, or if you get a combination, such as the *Big Four*, the 4-6-7-10, the best you can do is try for count unless you are inclined to believe in miracles. By count, I mean going for the pins that you have a reasonably good chance of converting. They will add to your score, whereas a total miss will hurt your score.

Let's suppose you strike on your first ball. However, you leave the 4-6-7-9-10 spare on the first ball of your next frame. That's an unusual leave that we call the *Greek Church*. You try for the spare—a difficult one—and you miss, perhaps going in the channel when you were trying to slide a pin over from the right side of the lane to take out the 4 and 7 on the left. You get 10 for your first frame strike plus five for the sum of your next two balls. That gives you a score of 15 in the first frame and 20 in the second.

However, had you played percentages, gone for the three pins on the right side of the lane, and converted them on your second shot, you would have received 10 plus 8, or 18, in the first frame and 26 in the next. That's six pins over what you collected for a brave—but foolish—attempt to convert a very difficult spare.

Try for the largest number pins you can reasonably expect to make on any difficult spare, unless it is late in the game and a conversion can mean a personal high game or the difference between victory and defeat. That's how I faced up to the 6-7-10 split in the Brunswick World Open I told you about earlier.

Remember, bowling, like many sports, is a game of inches. Inches mean the difference between a hit and a foul ball, an ace and an out, a basket and a rebound, or a spare and a miss.

Try my suggestions. If you find that they just aren't suited to your game, work out

PICKING UP SPARES . . . is the key to winning consistently. We pros must make 95 percent of our spares in order to survive tour competition.

your own calibrated system of moves and target arrows. I think, however, that most bowlers will find that my three-board basic adjustment on spare shooting will suit them well.

SLOW OR FAST?

You can get as many different opinions on the speed with which the spare ball should be thrown as there are pro bowlers. Most pros feel that the ball should be speeded up on spare shots. Some think the speed should be the same as on the strike ball. I believe it helps to speed up your spare shot because on a faster throw, particularly if you throw a pronounced hook as I do, the ball will hold a straighter line. I would never recommend slowing the ball down on your second shot.

It all depends upon the seriousness with which you take your bowling. If you bowl many games every week, experiment with speeding up your spare shots. However, if you are an average bowler, who plays once or twice a week, I'd suggest you deliver your spare ball with about the same velocity you strive for on your strike shot.

Johnny Petraglia, the left-hander who succeeded me in 1971 as Firestone Tournament of Champions winner, believes that taking as little time as possible on the approach results in a smaller margin of error. Petraglia virtually raced through the finals in the 1971 Tournament of Champions. It may have been the fastest he's ever bowled. He felt that going fast was his best bet; that standing there indecisively when he was all set would only increase his chances of being nervous and result in a poor shot.

I have to disagree with his approach, however. Although I would never advocate dallying on the approach, I feel you have to concentrate and take your time to make sure your feet move slowly and smoothly.

DOs AND DON'Ts

DO work hard to convert at least 80 percent of your spares.

DO study the way your ball drops off the end of the lane on your strike ball. It can tell you how much your ball is deflecting off the pins.

DO walk toward your target on all spare shots.

DO keep the same target on all spares but move your target on right-handed spares.

DO remember that, on all single-pin spares except for the 7- and 10-pins, you have a margin of error of over half the lane in which to make the spare. The ball is roughly 8½ inches wide, and the pin is 4¾ inches wide. You need only graze the pin on either side to knock it down, so you have a target area of almost 22 inches on the 41- or 42-inch-wide lane in which to succeed.

DON'T attempt to convert virtually impossible spares unless the game depends upon it. Always go for count.

DON'T speed up your spare shot. Keep it constant with your strike shot unless you are an advanced or pro bowler.

DON'T lose your concentration by allowing yourself to get angry over a split or leave on what seems to be a perfect strike ball. Spares are part of the game and must be accepted and mastered.

DON'T treat spares lightly. The outcome of a match or a good score will more often depend on your spares than on your strikes.

THE TRACK AREA . . . in most bowling houses is located somewhere between the ninth and fourteenth boards.

chapter 5
THE TRACK

The most discussed word in bowling today is the *track*, the depression or groove in the surface of the lane created by the thousands of balls that are rolled down the lane day after day.

Many once-a-week bowlers and even league bowlers think you are putting them on when you tell them about the track and its vagaries. But if you hope to improve your score or become a better-than-average bowler, you must conquer the track.

LANES CONDITIONING

To understand the mysteries of the track, you must understand how the lanes are conditioned, why they are conditioned, and how conditioning affects your game.

Obviously, under the constant impact and friction of 13- to 16-pound bowling balls, lanes would be reduced to kindling if they weren't protected in some way. That is why they are resurfaced and relacquered periodically and kept in condition with an oil substance.

American Bowling Congress rules used to stipulate that lanes had to be refinished once a year. Now, since harder plastic lacquers and lighter, more friction-resistant oils have been developed, the ABC allows an owner to refinish his lanes every two years.

But every year more bowlers are competing. Under this heavy play, the finishes still break down. Lanes can be put back into playable condition more easily and less expensively than before, but the breakdowns can cause some perplexing variations in the track area.

In a heavily played house, people bowling early in the day will often find the lanes in smoother, more playable condition than do those who compete late at night. It's similar to the problem pro golfers encounter. The early starters putt over smooth greens; the late starters must contend with all the spike marks left in the greens by those who played ahead of them.

Another vital factor in your game is the

amount of oil on the track. A dry lane allows you to hook your ball more easily, but the lane soon becomes pocked. The ideal lane will have a coating of oil spread just thin enough so that a hook can be obtained on a skillfully thrown ball.

Today most conditioning, like pinspotting, is done by machine. The machine is set to lay down a specified amount of oil on the lane. If distributed properly, the oil will be spread most heavily in the center of the lane, where play is the heaviest. The oil probably will be spread no more than 20 to 40 feet down-lane—the area in which the ball will be skidding and creating friction. Some oil will be carried farther downlane by the bowling balls, but it is the first 20 to 40 feet with which the bowler should be concerned. In a house used by many women and junior bowlers, the area may be reduced to about 20 feet, because such bowlers simply don't throw the ball hard enough the carry the oil down-lane.

There's been a lot of talk about "blocking" the lane—that is, using oil to create a pathway to the strike pocket. It is illegal. This kind of talk upsets me. Applying more oil to the center of the lanes, which I think is correct, may be illegal, but we've been doing it since my early days in the game in the 1950s. We used a spraygun then. Someone would walk down the lanes and spray oil on them. Most of the oil would be directed toward the center of the lane.

Now the machines can be set to apply more oil in a given spot than in another. While I don't believe that they should be set to be oil-heavy in the center and sand-dry on the outside, there should always be more oil in the center, because that's where heavy play is concentrated.

Personally, I don't like the new lanes applicators. They simply don't put enough oil on the lanes. The heads are often left almost bone-dry, and your ball hooks the minute you put it down. The machine puts oil down, but when it glides back up the lane it buffs all the oil off again. I wish they'd go back to the old spraygun method. I think it produced better lane conditions. But you can't stand in the way of progress, especially when it saves money.

A good lanes proprietor will adjust the oiling according to the needs of the bowlers. I don't mean the proprietor should doctor up the lanes to give some of the bowlers higher scores. But if most of the bowlers are average, less oil might be applied on the areas on which an unskilled bowler might roll. The lane would therefore be drier and more suited to the average bowler's hook. If the bowling house is used heavily by more skilled bowlers, the good proprietor will adjust accordingly. A modern bowling lane is a costly investment. The way an operator treats the lanes will be in direct relation to the maintenance costs. If the bowlers feel that the lanes are being given fair and consistent upkeep, the result will be better scores, more customer satisfaction, and good business.

On the pro tour, our lanes conditioning crew goes to a tournament house a month in advance and has the lanes recoated. They fix up the unruly track. On the pro tour, we use more oil on the lanes, because a pro puts more revolutions on the ball, and the friction eats up more oil.

In the normal, nontournament house, the janitor often takes care of conditioning the lanes. He might do the conditioning only once or twice a week or do it in an inconsistent manner. It is true that we pros have better playing conditions than most bowlers. In all sports, facilities are kept in top condition for the pros. Golf courses are manicured before major tournaments, and baseball players have ground crews to keep the playing surface in shape.

A LANES CONDITIONER . . . spreads oil as it moves up and down the lanes.

But even on the tour, the track conditions vary from house to house, and every bowler, even a pro, has to learn to adjust to lane conditions. Riviera Lanes in Akron, Ohio, site of the $125,000 Firestone Tournament of Champions, is well known as a high-scoring house. The pro tournament site in South Bend, Indiana, is another such establishment. It took a 247 average one year to win in South Bend. But in Winston-Salem, North Carolina, it took only a 202 average to make the finals.

No matter how the lanes are conditioned, humidity and temperature can make a big difference. On the pro tour, we usually find that scores on the East Coast segment of the tour are lower because of the salt water in the air and the humidity.

We pros have had a disagreement with the American Bowling Congress about our lanes conditioning program. Guess what?

The pros have had fewer 300 games since we started our lanes conditioning program than we did before. If we're trying to cheat, as has been intimated, why don't we have more 300 games? What we're really trying to do is make conditions as consistent as possible, so that tournament scores will more correctly reflect the skill of the players. Ideally, those are the conditions that should exist for every bowler, not just for the pros.

Still another factor in lanes conditioning is buffing. This, too, can be done either by machine or by hand. The buffing can be done either up and down the lanes or from side to side. The direction in which a lane is buffed can be of great importance to the advanced bowler. It can affect the direction of the ball as it rolls toward the strike pocket.

You probably think that I am getting

highly technical at this point. You are absolutely correct. If you're just bowling for a fun night out, all this discussion will seem overly detailed. But if you're a serious student of the game, you'll ask questions about the way the lanes are conditioned and apply what you've learned toward your game.

FINDING THE TRACK

In most bowling houses the track will be located between the 9th and 14th boards. That is the natural spot for most bowlers to attack the pocket. If you use the second target arrow as I have recommended, you'll probably be bowling within the track.

But finding the track does not automatically mean higher scores. If you're bowling on a lane that has recently been resurfaced, the track area will be only a small depression—almost an ideal condition. However, if the lane hasn't been resurfaced for two years, the track area may be deep, wide, and erratic because of heavy play. The bowling patterns of women bowlers, who tend to roll the ball straight down the middle of the lane, also affect your ball. You can imagine the problems you may encounter as you cross the track while shooting for spares.

On a lane with a pronounced track, it often is better to bowl outside the track to get a smoother surface. You may even find it necessary to switch your target arrow to the first or third arrow in extreme cases.

Our PBA lanes conditioning program has eliminated some of the worst inequities of the track. Before the program began, the left-handed pro bowlers often had better playing conditions because there was much less wear on the left side of the lanes. The left-handed bowlers were dominating many PBA events, and a great howl went up from their right-handed rivals.

Even now, when lanes conditioning has changed the situation, great left-handed bowlers such as Dave Davis are accused of having an unfair advantage. I don't think that's true—Dave would be just as great a bowler if he were right-handed. The charges upset him, I think.

In your house, however, it may still be true that left-handed bowlers have an advantage. But even they must find the track —its location is crucial for cross-alley spare shooting as well as for shooting strikes.

How do you find the track? The easiest way is to watch some of the high-average bowlers in your establishment. They'll know where it is, or they wouldn't be rolling those high scores. Ask them about the track. Or ask your proprietor. While you're at it, inquire how long it's been since the lanes were resurfaced.

Once you find the track, experiment. Observe what your ball does on various shots from different angles. Keep adjusting and trying again. That's the only way to learn how to beat the track. All I can give you, besides that general advice, are some tips for experimentation.

With some variations, you will probably find it necessary to attack the track from three different angles. Which angle you choose will depend primarily on how recently the lanes have been refinished.

If the lanes have been resurfaced recently, the track area may be nonexistent. The lanes will be very slick, and you will have to try what we pros call the "gutter shot" to master them. By gutter shot I mean a ball rolled at an extreme outside angle. Roll the ball over the first arrow, just five boards to the left of the channel. Begin seven boards to the right of normal strike position.

However, if the lanes haven't been resurfaced for six weeks to a year and a half, stick with the second target arrow, 10 boards from the right-hand channel. Normal play over the period will have resulted in a pronounced but fair track, somewhere between the 9th and 14th boards. You can exploit this track with a well-delivered shot.

Now, let's suppose you encounter a lane that hasn't been resurfaced for over a year and a half. You are in for real trouble because of the wear on it from men, women, and juniors, all throwing different kinds of balls with varying angles and degrees of hook.

The track may be so erratic that it would be best to avoid it altogether. Try a few practice shots. If the ball acts erratically on what seems to be a soundly delivered ball over the second arrow, you must adjust drastically to survive.

I would suggest that you use an inside angle to avoid the track area. Start with your left foot positioned at the 27th board. Put your ball out over the third arrow, which is 15 boards from the channel. The path of your ball should be on the inside edge of the well-worn track.

If the condition inside the track area is consistent, your ball will have a much better chance of hooking back and getting the strike pocket than it would if it were rolled down an erratic track. You may, however, find no luck on the inside angle and have to go back to the gutter shot—the first arrow—and get an outside angle on the unplayable track.

Locating the track is vital. But even once you've found it, it can be a godsend or a crucifixion. The amount of conditioning oil in the track, or on either side of it, can be a problem. Your only solution is to try the angles I have suggested and see which seems to work best.

Seek the truest condition possible on each lane. When your ball reacts the way it normally does, you know you've found the spot for you.

DOs AND DON'Ts

DO locate the track in your favorite house or in any house in which you are competing.

DON'T assume that once you have found the track you can always use it to make strikes.

DO look for the track between the 9th and 14th boards.

DO, if in doubt, observe high-average bowlers and ask them for the track's location.

DO consider three different angles of attack once you've located the track: the regular, inside, and outside angles, depending upon how recently the lanes have been resurfaced.

DON'T get perturbed if it takes you some time and practice to locate the track. It isn't easy to find or master. But think what an edge you'll have on everyone else when you do locate it!

A DELICATE SCALE . . . measures the ball's weight to within one-sixteenth of an ounce. Exact measurement is vital to the proper weighting and drilling of your ball.

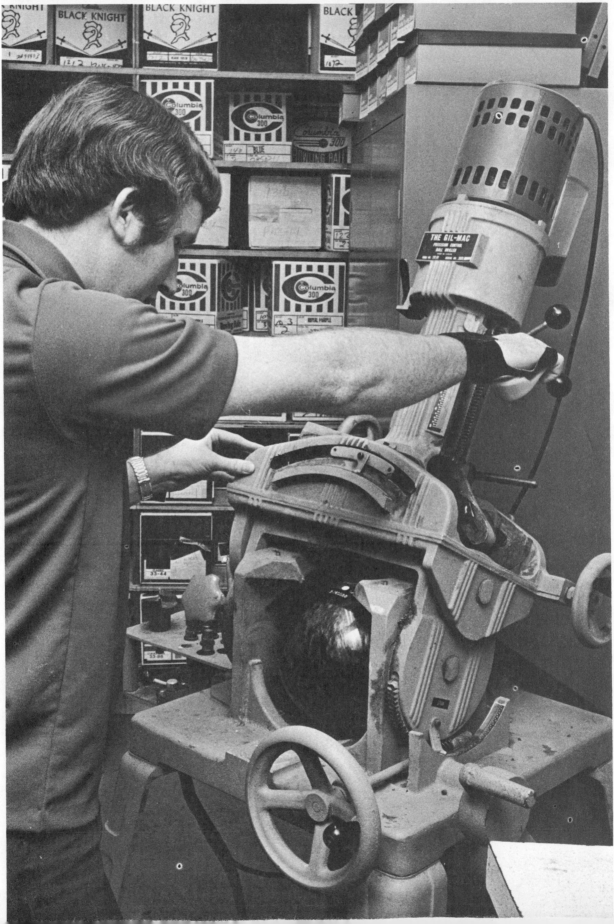

chapter 6
WEIGHT AND PITCH

The most revolutionary improvement in professional bowling is the adjustment of weight on the bowling ball itself. For years, no one ever thought that adding more weight to one side of the ball could produce dramatic improvements in one's game. You might have heard about ball weighting and thought about experimenting with it.

Tinkering with weight, however, is a highly technical part of bowling. No one should consider it unless he or she has reached a 180 average or over. Then, if your game is at an impasse you might try it —if you know a highly skilled ball-driller.

Many once-a-week bowlers never know that when they buy a ball it usually will have about three ounces more weight on the top than on the bottom. The total weight of the ball will be printed plainly on the carton in which it comes. The weight will be incorporated in a block under the surface of the ball, just under the serial number and brand name.

ABC rules allow the ball to be three ounces heavier on the top than on the bottom. The rules also allow one ounce of weight on the right or left side and one ounce of finger or thumb weight.

The combinations of weights are endless, but what we are essentially talking about is a possible shift of five ounces of weight— a considerable amount that can really help the action of your ball.

First, let's establish the reason you might want to adjust the weight of your ball: to govern at what point down-lane you want it to hook, and how much you want it to hook. In order to get the best insight into how and why a ball should be weighted, I went to Fred Borden, a PBA member who operates Eastgate Pro Lanes in Akron, Ohio. He is my "doctor." Whenever I go into a prolonged slump on tour, I hurry home to this excellent instructor to straighten me out. Over and above that, I believe Fred is the best ball-driller in the world.

Here is what Fred suggests on the delicate matter of weight adjustment:

"Every ball, when shipped from the manufacturer, will weigh between 16 pounds, 2 ounces and 16 pounds, 3½ ounces, before it is drilled. It is the 2 to 3½ ounces with which the ball-driller is allowed to play by ABC regulations, since no ball may weigh over 16 pounds in competition. It is the driller's job, through use of a delicate scale that can measure weight to within one-sixteenth of an ounce, to determine dead-center on the weight block so proper adjustment can be made when the ball is drilled for finger and thumb holes.

"As a rule of thumb, the driller, after determining dead-center as to weight distribution, will move one-half inch left, right, forward, or back of dead-center to distribute weight to suit an individual bowler's style. Let's suppose you are in the advanced stage of bowling with a high average. Far too often, however, you don't get up to the pocket, so you leave a lot of 5-pins on seemingly well-rolled shots.

"What you may need is right side and finger weight. By that I mean an ounce more weight on the right side of the ball and an ounce more in front of the finger holes. This weight adjustment will cause the

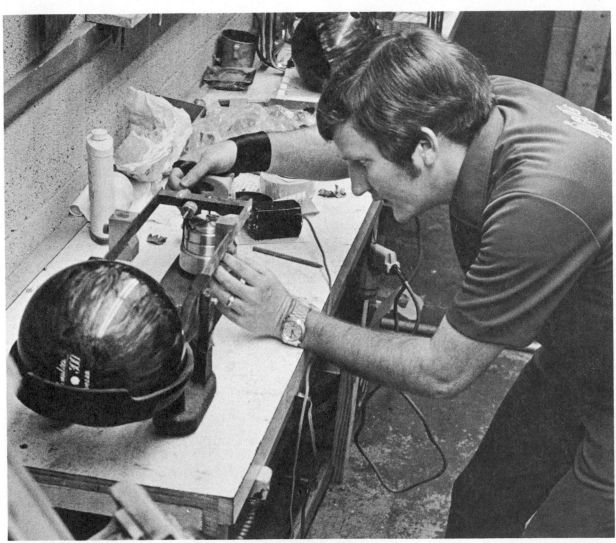

A SKILLED BALL-DRILLER . . . will use this machine to shift the weight of your ball from one side to another when he drills the finger and thumb holes.

ball to skid much farther down-lane before it starts to hook and then, taking the right side weight, snap into the pocket with more authority. You would apply such weight by moving one-half inch to the left and down from dead-center and drilling your finger and thumb holes. Thus the top-weight of your ball would be reduced and an ounce shifted forward and right on the ball.

"Suppose you find you are bothered by a ball that hooks too quickly and constantly strikes the head pin, too high or too solidly. You may need negative weight. What you need now is left-side and thumb weight. We accomplish this in just the opposite manner as before. The ball-driller will move a half-inch right and up from dead-center of the weight block and drill your finger and thumb holes in that position.

"Now your ball will have less weight on the left and front than before. Your shot will tend to hook more quickly after release but will tend to straighten out and snuggle into the pocket on impact.

"If you are a 150-average bowler, don't get involved in weights. The top-weight already built into your ball most likely will help you deliver a good hook.

"The possible weight combinations are endless. For Don Johnson, because of his big hook, I have programmed use of three-quarters-ounce finger weight and one-quarter-ounce right-side weight. This weight suits Don best because he uses a lot of instinct and twist on his release, a style advisable only for the pro or very advanced bowler. The average bowler should always keep his wrist locked in at the 10 o'clock position and execute the conventional delivery."

What type of ball you throw will definitely affect what weights will do for your game. The average bowler doesn't understand that most delivered balls fall into three categories—*full-roller, semi-roller* and *spinner*.

After you have rolled the ball several times, look at it. The ball will have a decided ring around it caused by the oil and grime on the lanes. This allows you to determine what type of ball you are throwing. (See Diagram 26.) If the ring defines a circle around the middle of the ball, between the thumb and finger holes, you are throwing a full-roller, the easiest ball for the average bowler to control.

If you are throwing a semi-roller, the track on your ball will be clearly defined below the thumb hole. This means that probably, without knowing it, you turned your bowling hand ever so slightly at point of release.

The spinner is the hardest ball for the average bowler to control, but it is a boon for the pros. The ball will revolve on a very

DIAGRAM 26

FULL-ROLLER

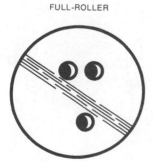

SEMIROLLER

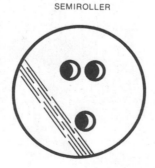

SPINNER

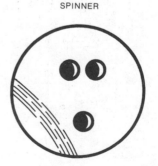

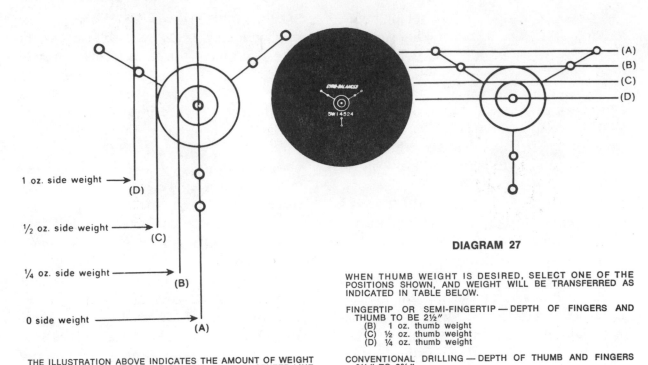

1 oz. side weight ———→ (D)

½ oz. side weight ———→ (C)

¼ oz. side weight ———————→ (B)

0 side weight ————————————→ (A)

THE ILLUSTRATION ABOVE INDICATES THE AMOUNT OF WEIGHT TRANSFERRED TO THE RIGHT SIDE OF GRIP WHEN CENTER LINE IS MOVED TO LEFT OF CENTER.

NOTE: For left-hand grip, move the center line to the right of center to accomplish the same effect.

DIAGRAM 27

WHEN THUMB WEIGHT IS DESIRED, SELECT ONE OF THE POSITIONS SHOWN, AND WEIGHT WILL BE TRANSFERRED AS INDICATED IN TABLE BELOW.

FINGERTIP OR SEMI-FINGERTIP — DEPTH OF FINGERS AND THUMB TO BE 2½"
   (B)   1 oz. thumb weight
   (C)   ½ oz. thumb weight
   (D)   ¼ oz. thumb weight

CONVENTIONAL DRILLING — DEPTH OF THUMB AND FINGERS 2½" TO 2¾".
   (A)   1 oz. thumb weight
   (B)   ¾ oz. thumb weight
   (C)   ½ oz. thumb weight
   (D)   ¼ oz. thumb weight

small circumference. It takes a lot of instinct and wrist-snap to get it down pat. If you can make instant adjustments with your wrist, you get a weak hook ball, but one that has a great deal of accuracy.

Pros now advise the semi-roller for most advanced bowlers. The reason is that, while the ball rolls smoothly, it does have some added twist on it and is not too difficult for an advanced bowler to master.

Diagram 27 shows how the Ebonite company weights its Gyro-Balanced ball. As you can see, weighting is a complex process that can only be done by experts.

Please, don't go experiment with positive and negative weights for your ball unless you have reached the advanced stage. If you reach that point, consult an expert ball-driller or pro. An ounce here or there can be worth a pound of pins for your game, but only if the weight is distributed properly by

an expert driller.

PITCH

This is another highly technical area with which the average bowler usually should not concern himself. Finger and thumb holes drilled into a ball need not necessarily go straight down. They can be angled to provide a bowler with a better grip and more confidence when he or she releases the shot.

The average bowler will want his finger holes drilled straight down in the center-weight position of his ball. But there may be exceptions. An office worker who has a weak wrist may need to have his thumb and finger holes pitched in toward the center of the ball to provide a more secure grip. This can be paramount for women or junior bowlers who have difficulty when all the weight of the ball is on their arm or fingers.

But say you are dealing with a construction worker or laborer who has strong fingers and wrists. Such a bowler might pitch the finger and thumb holes away from center to avoid overpowering the ball. Your fingers may also have some special structural characteristics that will necessitate a different pitch. Consult your pro.

An instant after observing your release, the pro will be able to suggest ideas that may correct flaws in your game. The pro may talk to you about pitch or weighting of the ball. In this case, consider it seriously—he would not even suggest it if he did not feel it would help improve your average.

But just because I and other members of the Professional Bowlers Association tour experiment with weighting the ball, don't think it is a cureall for your bowling ills. Unless you know how to handle it, experimentation in this area can be disasterous.

Only the advanced bowler should attempt to deal with this subject.

DOs AND DON'Ts

DO stay with the conventional top weight built into your bowling ball until you become a better-than-average bowler.

DO, if you are an advanced bowler, ask your lanes pro to study your game to determine if shifting weights on your ball might improve your average.

DO determine what type of ball you are throwing—full, semi-roller, or spinner. You might want to develop a new delivery to help your game.

DON'T overlook changing the pitch of your finger holes if you are having trouble holding or controlling the ball.

DON'T make any changes in weight or pitch without having your lanes pro or an advanced bowler study your game first.

JUNIOR BOWLERS . . . are getting better all the time, thanks to organized junior bowling programs. Before long these pupils of mine may be breaking my records on the pro tour — or at least bowling the highest scores in their leagues.

chapter 7
SPECIAL TIPS

The bowling techniques I've talked about in this book can be used by any bowler, regardless of age, sex, or physical characteristics. But some bowlers do have special problems, and I'd like to deal with them in this chapter.

THE WOMAN BOWLER

Without doubt, a woman's biggest problem is that she finds it difficult to throw a ball that hooks. This problem exists mainly because a woman's arms are physically different from those of a man. When a woman's forearm is extended, it tends to turn outward, while a man's forearm is relatively straight. To compensate for this difference in bone structure, it is essential that a woman make an extra effort to keep her thumb in the 9, 10, or 11 o'clock position at the point of release.

What happens far too often is that a woman chooses a ball that is too heavy for her to handle. The heavy ball makes her wrist collapse on delivery. Although she

may start with her thumb in the 10 o'clock position, the weight of the ball and her arm structure cause her to release the ball in such a manner that she gets a *backup ball.*

A backup ball happens when the wrist collapses at point of release. The thumb is then positioned on top of the ball, and the bowler doesn't get the lift and twist that will produce the desired hook. Instead, the ball backs up: it starts toward the pins, but then fades away in the wrong direction.

The backup ball is a weak one that just won't get the mixing action of a ball that hooks. You'll see a lot of women throwing backup balls in average league play, but you'll very seldom see a woman in an advanced league throwing one.

You'll find as you improve that bowling is a sport in which women can become almost as proficient as men. In a short series of games, a woman can match or sometimes better a man's score. I've lost some exhibition games to woman pros. But

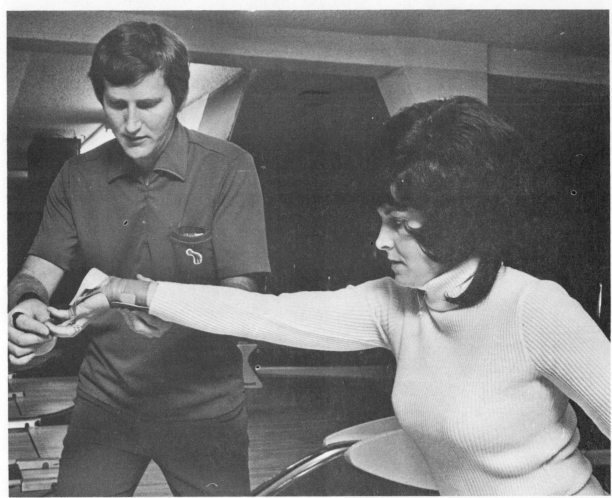

IT'S ALL TOO EASY . . . for a woman to turn her wrist out, since her forearm turns outward naturally. If she releases the ball with her wrist turned like this, instead of in the 10 o'clock position, she'll throw a backup ball instead of a hook.

DOTTY FOTHERGILL

LOA BOXBERGER

over an extended period, a woman's strength usually gives out before the man's.

A woman's second biggest problem is that, because she lacks strength, she also may lack control in her delivery. I talked to two top woman bowlers, Loa Boxberger and Dotty Fothergill, about this and other problems of woman bowlers.

"To be a good bowler," said Dotty Fothergill, "a woman must have a good instructor. She must forget about being dainty and feminine on the lanes. She must get speed on her delivery. She must get a good arm swing and bend her right knee so that she can get leverage on the ball when she releases it.

"Most women have more rhythm and grace than men. Those attributes are to her advantage in this game. But the woman bowler just can't forget that she must also get some power into her delivery with the heaviest possible ball. A lighter ball will deflect too much off the pins if it isn't delivered with some velocity."

Loa Boxberger agreed, "A lot of women bowlers know exactly what their problem is. It's lack of power and leverage on release. A big problem for the average woman is that she doesn't get her right leg bent properly on the third step. When she reaches the fourth step and slides, she's in an awkward position, off balance and unable to impart any speed to the ball."

Even with more speed, however, a good, solid ball can't be obtained unless a woman keeps her wrist locked in with her thumb in that 10 o'clock position. With legs bent, she should reach out strongly for her target, almost as if she wanted to shake hands with it.

A woman must always remember to keep her hand at the gripping position on the *side* of the ball, not underneath it. It's the only way she can ever develop any type of hook and get away from the backup ball blues.

Another problem for women bowlers is that far too many of them don't get enough backswing on the approach. A woman might be afraid of dropping the ball and hold her arm stiff, instead of letting the

GET THAT RIGHT LEG BACK . . . and bend your knees for added power when you release the ball. Mary Ann demonstrates the perfect position for a woman bowler and then rolls a ball that just has to be a strike.

LET THE BALL DROP NATURALLY . . . from the pushaway position, and don't be afraid you're going to drop it. The weight of the ball will give you added power on your backswing.

ball's weight carry her arm down naturally into a powerful backswing. Letting the ball drop naturally on the second step gets the arm back farther and in a stronger position for the release when a bowler comes forward for the fourth step and slide.

THE JUNIOR BOWLER

I'll be honest and tell you I don't plan on letting my son bowl—even if he wants to—until he is eight years old. I think that if a youngster starts any earlier than that the ball is just too heavy and he may develop bad habits.

Of course, it all depends upon how advanced in growth the boy or girl is. Some eight-year-olds are well developed. I think Little League baseball has proved that some very young boys are much stronger than others and can become overpowering pitchers or hitters because of their physical attributes.

There are two very large junior bowling programs in the United States, the Youth Bowling Association and the American Junior Bowling Congress programs. In some instances, the children are permitted to throw 6-pound balls instead of the normal ABC regulation of 8 pounds.

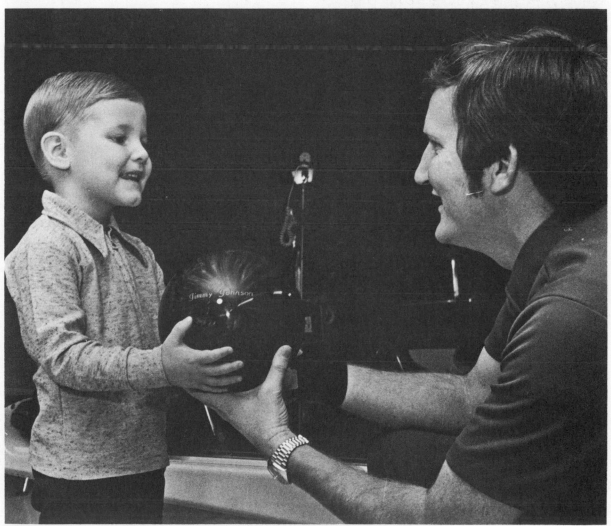

MY SON JIMMY . . . has his own ball, but he won't be bowling until he's eight years old. The ball is too heavy for a toddler, and Jimmy could develop bad habits trying to handle it.

The 6 pounders are for boys and girls who are very small in stature. For the normal 8- to 10-year-old, I recommended the 8-pound ball.

The junior league program is fantastic in developing future stars of our game. That's how I got started. The instructors are exceptional and the nation's bowling lanes owners are very tolerant, because they realize that these youngsters are their future customers.

One of my first jobs as full-time bowler was being an instructor for young bowlers in Crawfordsville, Indiana. We had a school bus that picked up the children after school and delivered them to the lanes for my instruction. Seeing some of the boys and girls move on to good league averages when they became older was very rewarding.

The most common problem any junior bowler encounters is a tendency to try to overpower the ball, which is hard for him to handle in the first place. Children tend to run up to the foul line and try to throw the ball too hard and too fast. They must be taught to keep their feet slow.

If they run up to the foul line, they will be off balance, with no timing. They'll be thrown to the right on their delivery and they'll have absolutely no direction.

When I graduated from high school, I already had set my mind on becoming a pro bowler. I was averaging about 165 a game. Now I see young people averaging 200 when they are 15 and 210 when they are 16. That's a pretty good endorsement of the junior bowling program.

Today a youngster can, through this organized, instructional program, be a 200-average bowler by the time he is in high school. That's why the competition on the pro tour today is so difficult. The kids keep coming out of the walls and challenging us. And they are good bowlers, solidly grounded in the right approach to the game.

A word of advice, however, learned by hard experience. If you are a 198 to 202-average league bowler, I don't think you've got a chance on the pro tour.

There have been bowlers who averaged 220 in league play, came on the tour, and couldn't make it. Why? Because in league play, you are bowling on the same lanes each time out. On the pro tour, you keep switching lanes for each game, and you keep switching houses from week to week. You will find a different surface each game and each week. That's a big difference.

THE OVERWEIGHT BOWLER

An overweight person can have some problems using the area bowling concept. He or she may have to lay the ball down farther away from the left ankle than would a thinner bowler. I still don't recommend laying the ball down more than eight boards from the left ankle, but in some cases it may be the only answer to a bulging waistline.

I would also suggest that overweight bowlers don't address the pins with the ball held directly in front of them. It would be better to set up with the ball held in line with the bowling shoulder. That will enable a heavy bowler to go more directly into his arm swing without having to wrap the ball around the hips, an act that usually will result in a pulled shot.

Do, however, remember to really keep the elbow tucked in as close to your waist as possible on the armswing. With the ball already held to the outside rather than in the center, a free-swinging elbow could throw off your whole shot.

DOs AND DON'Ts

DO, if you are a woman, try to develop a ball that hooks.

DO, if you are a woman, work on getting

your right leg fully bent on the third step of the delivery.

DON'T, if you are a woman, let your wrist collapse on delivery or allow your thumb to be positioned on top of the ball instead of in the 10 o'clock position.

DO, if you are a woman, let your ball's weight carry your arm down and into the backswing. The resulting more powerful backswing will help you put more muscle into the ball.

DO, if you are a junior bowler, try to keep your feet slow on your approach.

DO, if you are overweight, try holding the ball, at the address position, in line with the bowling shoulder.

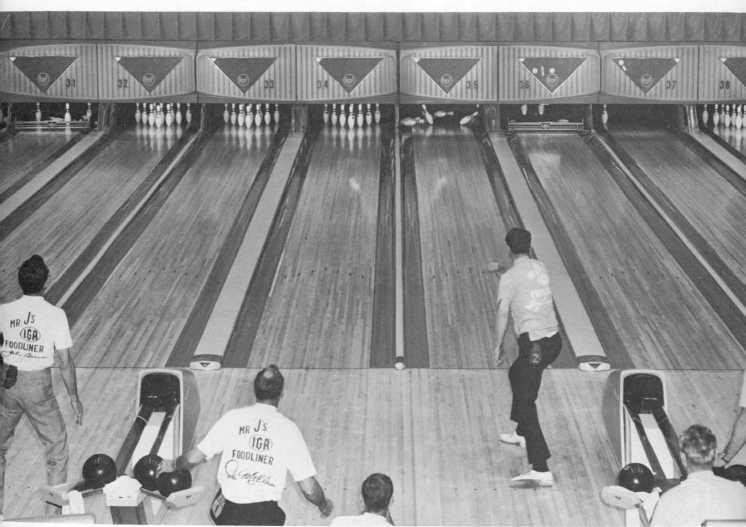

LEAGUE BOWLING . . . gives every bowler the chance to bowl in competition.
The excitement of competing will add to your enjoyment of the game.

chapter 8
COMPETITIVE BOWLING

I seldom get a chance to bowl in league play any more because of the **PBA** tour format, which consists mainly of two-man, head-to-head play. But amateur bowling concentrates on team play, and I imagine that's how you'll be doing most of your bowling.

You'll enjoy league play. You'll get to meet a lot of people. Bowling is a great mixer. In leagues the accent is on good fellowship and relaxation. That's the way it should be. Team play adds the excitement of competition to bowling—you'll get a special thrill when you make a key strike or tough spare that helps your team to victory.

The more advanced the league gets, the more serious competition will become. You probably will find it harder to concentrate in the high-average league because the play is slower and the distractions are more prevalent. But the rewards in enjoyment will make the extra work worthwhile.

There are a variety of leagues in which you can bowl. The most common is the five-man or woman team league. There are also singles and doubles leagues, mixed leagues for men and women, father and son, and mother and daughter leagues. Ordinarily, the first league you join will be a five-player team league, quite often with a group of people in your club or with whom you work or go to church.

Don't be concerned about your ability. The league probably will operate on a handicap system, which will tend to equalize all teams in the championship race.

Each bowler on your team will have an average. By ABC rules, averages are established on the basis of 21 games. The total number of pins you knock down in your first 21 games each season will be used to determine your average.

The averages of each member of your team will be added, as will those of your opponents. The ABC recommends a handicap of 75 percent. If your team had a 750 average and was matched against a team with an 850 average, your team would receive a 75-pin handicap on each game.

Your team will have a captain, whose decision on your team lineup can be important. Usually the team member who has the highest average will be placed in the *fifth position*. This bowler is the *anchor*. As the game nears its end and you need vital strikes or spares, the anchor man is like the cleanup hitter in baseball.

Your second best bowler should begin the game. Your third best bowler will be fourth, your next best second and your weakest, or lowest average bowler, will be third. This arrangement gets you balance —your two best scorers are at the top and the bottom, where they can pick the team up on crucial shots.

If your place of employment, church, or club doesn't sponsor a bowling league, don't despair. Just check with the proprietor of your lanes. Almost every league has openings to fill up teams before the season starts in August, so the proprietor can find a team on which you can bowl, whose members will welcome you.

Businesses of all types have proved to be the backbone of league bowling. Businesses sponsor teams and, in many cases, entire leagues. A business that sponsors your team will usually pay your team's entry fee and provide you with a shirt or a uniform with the company's name on the back.

If a business sponsors an entire league, it will pay the entry fees of all of the teams, and the league will bear the name of the firm, giving it publicity in bowling reports in the newspapers or on radio and television.

The most important person in any league is its secretary. He or she will apply to the local bowling association for certification by the ABC. Each league member will receive an ABC membership card. The ABC offers awards for 300 games and other scoring feats. Your membership card

entitles you to compete for these awards and also to enter any tournament under the ABC's jurisdiction.

For men, the largest tournament is the national ABC tournament, which attracts 5,000 or more teams annually and lasts several months. It has divisions for high- and low-average teams and for professional bowlers. Its counterpart for women is the Women's International Bowling Congress (WIBC) tournament.

For many bowlers the ABC or WIBC tournament is the highlight of the bowling season. It always is conducted in a major city, and teams plan two or three-day trips to compete in it. I've never heard of a team that returned from either of these tournaments unhappy, even if the players did not bowl well. The fellowship and thrill of competing in the event supersedes any disappointment on the lanes.

The local bowling association will also send your secretary a copy of the ABC rules, with ABC's suggested organization for each type of league. ABC rules may also be obtained from American Bowling Congress National Headquarters, 5301 South 76th Street, Greendale, Wisconsin 53129.

The secretary's toughest job will be computing averages. These must be posted weekly just before the league starts its play, so that handicaps may be determined. Each week after you have competed, the secretary will gather the results and draw up the standings of the teams. Usually, the secretary will be paid a small fee from league funds.

Every league will have a prize fund made up of a small portion of the fee you'll pay each week before you start to play. At the end of the year, the fund will be split according to how the teams fared in the standings. There is often a banquet where prizes are awarded for high game, high series, high average, and so on.

Ordinarily, your team will receive one point for each game won. The normal match is three games against a given opponent. A fourth point will be awarded to the team with the highest total score for all three games, handicap pins included. Occasionally, teams will tie in a game. In this case, each team gets one-half of a point.

While the five-man or woman team league is the most common, other types of leagues are gaining in popularity. Two of the most popular types are the mixed leagues and the father-son, mother-daughter leagues.

These are usually two-player teams. Small companies, which may not have enough employees for five-player leagues, often form employee-wife or employee-husband leagues. Mixed leagues for single men and women also are popular. Father-son, mother-daughter leagues are growing in popularity because of the excellent chance they give parents and children to relax and do things together.

Walk into any bowling lane during the afternoon hours and you will see it crowded by leagues composed of women, most of them housewives. Since many modern lanes offer nurseries or play centers for toddlers, a housewife can relax from her daily chores and at the same time enjoy the light exercise the game provides.

GAME STRATEGY

Once you decide what type of league suits you best, you must plan your game strategy. I believe that the best strategy is the old football coach's adage: "The best defense is a good offense."

Your team must attack from the first frame, and I think the one way to get the attack going is with team spirit. Cheer your teammates on with chatter and back-slapping. Your show of confidence will get everyone's adrenalin flowing. It's just got

to help your game to have someone rooting you on.

Won't all this chatter detract from your ability to concentrate? Not if it's done at the proper time. All the best teams on which I have bowled had great team spirit. But the rooting stopped when a player was on the approach. The bowler knew that this was the time to bear down and try to justify the team's confidence.

An all-important tip to remember is that the key to being a winning team is make your spares. We pros figure we'll average one open frame per game, because of either a split or an error. The average bowler probably will average two or more open frames. As in singles bowling, you must strive to convert as many spares as possible. On difficult spares or splits, always go for count unless making the tough shot means a last-frame victory. You must try to make it then.

The principle of going for the count is especially important in team play. Let's say you leave some tough three-pin spare shots. By trying to convert, you risk leaving two of the pins. By playing it safe, you can pick up two pins and leave only one. A good example would be the 6-7-10 split. If you try to slide a pin over to take out that pesky 7-pin, you may roll the ball too far to the right and miss both the 6 and the 10 by going into the channel, losing all three pins. Or you might misfire and get only the 6 or the 10 in your desire to get the 7, thus losing two pins. If you have two such situations per game and don't go for the count you could lose at least four pins. If each of your teammates does the same, your team has lost 20 points.

You might make a really difficult split once every 50 tries. It's a great thrill. But you've probably lost over 60 pins on your 49 misses—pins that could have added greatly to your average. I guarantee that

A MEMBER OF THE OPPOSING TEAM . . . is rooting for the bowler at the right to make a strike. That's the kind of spirit and enthusiasm you'll find in league competition.

you'll take home more loot and trophies if you always go for the count on tough pickups.

Another bit of advice that you will find invaluable is not to get upset by bench-jockeying from your rivals. Usually, it will all be good-natured kidding and part of the evening's fun. But if you are bowling badly you might tend to take it seriously and let it shatter your confidence. If your rivals see that you are cracking, they aren't going to stop. So laugh it off, even if it's getting to you.

Remember that in league bowling you can beat a better bowler because you'll have a higher handicap working for you. If you can bowl up to your average or over it, you've got a good chance to beat the better player. Don't be awed or beaten before you match up with someone who has a higher

average than yours. He or she has to roll up to average that night, too, or you will win.

On a good night, the lowest average team in your league can beat the highest average team. Look at the standings after a few weeks and you'll often see a middle-average team leading the league while the high-average team is down the standings. The middle-average team has been exceeding its averages, while the hotshots haven't been bowling up to their capabilities.

You'll hear a lot about "out-psyching" your opponents in competitive bowling. You're always going to run into some player who's your equal in ability but whom you somehow just never seem to be able to defeat. You may think there is something he does to " out-psych" you. But I prefer to think that you have just lost confidence in your own ability. Stop thinking about being hexed and roll your natural game. If you are convinced your game is good enough to win, you'll start winning, especially with your teammates cheering you on.

An article about me once said that I practiced "psyching" on the PBA tour. The article charged that I'd go up to an opponent just before a game and moan about my inability to find the angle on the lanes we were about to use. This made the other fellow think, "Gee, he's bowling well and he doesn't know the angle! Maybe I don't either." That article really made me mad. I've never done things like that. I don't believe in trying to destroy an opponent's confidence. I don't think any of the pros do.

Dave Davis is sometimes accused of trying to psych his opponents when he refuses to watch them bowl. Dave will sit during a match and never watch his rival throw the ball. But Dave isn't trying to unsettle his rival. He's simply trying to bolster his own concentration and calm his emotions. He believes that if he watches a rival throw a couple of garbage strikes, while he hasn't been getting any breaks during the game, it will ruin his confidence. It's as simple as that.

I've heard people say Dick Weber psychs his rivals with his confident, almost cocky, air. I don't know about that. All I know is that Dick Weber is simply the greatest at jumping on a rival. For example, if he is trailing and his opponent leaves an open frame, Dick will jump up and quickly throw a double. Pow! He's now 20 pins ahead. I don't call that psyching. I call it confidence in his own ability. That's why he is a great champion.

DOs AND DON'Ts

DO join a league for maximum enjoyment of the game.

DO remember that the best defense is a good offense.

DO go for the count on all difficult spares except in critical situations.

DO remember that your handicap is an equalizing factor. You can beat a better bowler if you just bowl up to your average —and he doesn't.

DON'T do your rooting when another bowler is on the approach.

DON'T get upset by bench-jockeying from the opposing team.

DON'T try to psych your opponent. You can do better by just bowling your own game and having confidence in yourself.

MY CONCENTRATION . . . is so great that I'm not even aware of the spectators. All I can think about is making those strikes. I'm so involved in what I'm doing that I unconsciously follow the ball with my body — I "run out" my strikes.

chapter 9
MENTAL ATTITUDE

I think there are several pro bowlers who are technically better than I am. They have technique and natural ability that I just can't match. Yet I have been able to beat them because of two intangible assets that I possess: desire and concentration.

Most people don't bowl for a living as I do; they bowl for fun and relaxation. But they still need desire and concentration if they're going to improve. You can't have concentration unless you've got desire. You've got to want to win every competition, whether it is a "beer frame" in your weekly bowling league session or the $125,000 Firestone Tournament of Champions.

Football coaches have a way of saying it: You've got to pay the price. Hard work, practice, dedication. That's what it takes to be a good bowler.

Unless you have exceptional talent and supreme will-power and are determined to be a pro, don't let the game become a monkey on your back. It's too much fun.

Work at bowling, but don't become a slave to it. Believe me, a 150-average bowler who rolls an occasional 200 game can derive just as much satisfaction from his performance as can a pro who wins a big tournament on national TV. It isn't the money but the sense of accomplishment that really counts.

Bowling can be great therapy after a rough working day. On your way to the lanes, think about the fact that now you are going to be able to relax and unwind. If you bowl badly, it will just be an extension of what already has been a miserable day. So set your mind on having a good game. This is something you can control. There will be no supervisors dictating what you must or must not do. Your success or failure will be based strictly on your decisions and your ability to solve problems.

On the bowling lanes, you are your own boss. Sometimes, your judgment will be correct and sometimes it won't. But it is your choice: if you miss an easy spare, you

MY LUCKY GOLD COINS . . . helped me win the 1970 Firestone Tournament of Champions. Mary Ann holds the coins while I'm bowling. You may think lucky charms don't work — but a lot of the pros use them to bolster their confidence and win games.

have no one to blame but yourself.

That's one of the pleasures of bowling. You are out there alone and no one is going to hinder your performance, except the most important person of all—you. If you can beat yourself, you can beat anyone.

CONCENTRATION

As I've said, concentration goes hand in hand with desire. I think golfer Gary Player is an excellent example of someone who has both. Player, the little South African, doesn't have the natural ability or strength of Jack Nicklaus or Arnold Palmer. But Player's desire and tremendous concentration have enabled him to battle Nicklaus and Palmer all the way for the top prizes in their profession.

If you've watched any of our nationally televised tournaments, I'm sure you've wondered how the pros are so calm, cool, and collected with the crowd roaring behind them, the TV lights blinding them, and thousands of dollars at stake.

It's hard to explain. I think each of the pros has his own secrets to keep his heart from rising into his throat. I'm famous for my trances, as I like to call them.

When I'm bowling well, I can shut distraction out of my mind so completely that absolutely nothing will rattle me. How do I do it? It's quite simple. I just attach a special emphasis to three parts of my game. I think about my feet. That's right, I said feet. I concentrate on making the first two steps of my delivery extra slow, smooth, and fluid. Then I concentrate on getting the ball out over the foul line with good lift and extension. Finally, I concentrate on making a full follow-through.

With all that on my mind, there is little room for distraction. I think someone could shoot off a cannon next to me and I wouldn't flinch a bit. I know that my wife often has thought of coming up between games of an important match and trying to encourage me. But she knows I'd never even recognize her when I'm in one of my trances.

POSITIVE THINKING

In my early days on the tour, I was so easily

discouraged that if I was bowling badly, I had no chance. I never considered that the leaders could hit a cold spell and I could catch up if I'd start doing things correctly.

Of course, lane conditions must favor your ball if you are to catch up from behind. After that it's simply a problem of making yourself perform to your capabilities.

Sometimes, no matter how hard you try, conditions will be stacked against you. Even then you should never give up. This point was driven home to me in 1971. Three times I won tournaments when, with only eight games remaining, victory seemed impossible.

It happened first at Redwood City, California. With eight games to go, I was 199 pins out of first place. But I got going in the stretch and won by 188 pins—I picked up 387 pins on the leader in just eight games. In the Waukegan Open, I was in even worse shape, 320 pins behind the leader, Tommy Tuttle. I won that one by 80 pins, so I picked up 400 pins on Tommy in the final eight games. My third spectacular rally was at the Brunswick World Open where I made that 6-7-10 split in the playoff to beat Larry Laub and clinch Bowler of the Year honors. With eight games to go, I was 400 pins out of second place. But I picked up all those pins to finish second, tied Larry in the title game, and then won in the playoff.

Dr. Norman Vincent Peale would have loved me because, after those comebacks, I'm a booster of the power of positive thinking. If you think you can, you have a chance. If you think you can't, you've already lost.

No matter how hard you try to concentrate, you'll come up against certain bowlers, conditions, and mental blocks that will seem impossible to defeat.

I know from experience that Mike McGrath always seems to beat me in head-to-head play. Conversely, I seem to have a hex on Dick Weber, one of the game's great match play artists. Good bowling has to exist in your head. No matter how technically proficient you are, much of your final score will be dictated by your mental approach to the game.

If lane conditions don't suit your ball, you can't just give up. You must try to find some way to counteract the conditions. If you are up against a bowler who seems to own you, try to put him out of your mind and bowl your regular game, which will probably be good enough to win.

THE CHOKING POINT

Taking the pipe, clutching, gassing, the big apple—all these derogatory terms mean that an athlete has let nerves ruin his or her performance under pressure. How do you counteract the feeling of numbness in your arms, lead in your feet, pounding in your heart, dryness in your throat, and twitching in your hand when you are shooting the key frame of your game, a frame that can mean victory or defeat or a personal high game?

The best advice I can suggest is to develop a "game plan." Develop a TV camera in your head. Plan just how you will deliver each ball on each lane.

You can't wait until you're on the approach to do this. You must plan the problems of changing lane conditions hours in advance. Talk to yourself. Tell yourself just how you'll confront each situation. Program yourself to react to a certain situation automatically.

Get to the lanes about 15 minutes before you are scheduled to bowl. Run over your game plan briefly in your mind. Then relax until it is time to start the game.

If you have prepared, your heart won't flutter nearly as much when you take to the lanes. Don't second-guess yourself. You

BODY ENGLISH . . . is the best way to release pent-up emotions during a crucial game. Almost every bowler uses it. Here, three pros in action.   Don Johnson, Dave Davis, and Marty Piriano.

have thought out your best plan of attack; stick with it.

Think strikes. Don't settle for second best on your mental approach. Certainly, you will have to convert spares during the game. But you'll wind up having to convert many more spares if you allow yourself to rely on the second chance instead of concentrating on the first opportunity to knock down all the pins.

Concentration on a predetermined game plan should enable you to block out all distractions. However, if the jitters still get you, take a deep breath just before you are about to deliver the ball. It will do wonders in breaking the tension that can build up on a critical shot. Above all, accept the crowd, if there is one. Even though I'm in a trance, I hear the fans and they rev me up.

You might also develop a personal quirk that gives you confidence when you are at the choking point. Personally, I'm a great believer in superstition. If I find I'm bowling well, for example, I may return and sit on the same spot on the bench where I've been sitting on previous strikes.

Let me tell you the story of the gold coins in 1970. I had been bowling badly for some time. Some friends in New Orleans gave me some old gold coins on the eve of the New Orleans Open. I won the tournament. My wife, Mary Ann, kept those coins in her purse and held them when I was bowling the next week in the Firestone Tournament of Champions. I won the tournament's $25,000 first prize.

I'm also a great believer in lucky colors. In the Fall of 1971, when I won all those tournaments that gave me Bowler of the Year honors, I always wore a burnt orange shirt and brown pants in the TV finals. My wife always wore something predominantly red. The PBA television director kept pleading for me to wear something different from week to week for color TV.

But I refused—and I kept winning. Even now, Mary Ann seldom wears anything blue when she watches me compete. I always seem to bowl badly when she wears that color.

In 1969 Jim Godman won the first place in the Firestone Tournament of Champions. His wife told everyone that she had known he would win before the first ball was ever rolled: she was clutching an old $2 bill throughout the tournament for good luck.

All this may sound silly, but I think it's part of the psychology of the game. These little things give me confidence, and that's what it takes to win.

Controlling Your Temper

Being able to control my temper on the lanes is another of my strong suits. The tension builds and it gets pretty wild out there at times.

I must admit I was pretty wild myself when I came out on the tour in 1964. The worst thing I ever did was in Colorado City in 1966. I had just thrown a game where I had buried every ball in the strike pocket and shot only 167. I was so mad that, when the ball came back on the return, I grabbed it and threw it as if it were a shot put.

A fellow pro was standing at the extreme left-hand side of the adjoining lane, shooting the 10-pin. My ball went right over his head. This scared and shocked me. I thought of how stupid I really was to almost have killed or seriously injured a friend because of a fit of temper.

I decided right there and then that I had to control my temper. Every day on the pro tour, I see players getting mad and absolutely throwing pins away in fits of anger. They can leave the solid 10-pin and be so upset that they won't take any time on the conversion, so they blow the spare.

Of course, you can't leave your pent-up emotions inside of you. There must be some way to release them or they will eventually destroy you. I'm told I release tension by "running out" my strikes. I don't notice that I'm doing it—I concentrate so hard that I am seldom conscious of how I finish after a critical shot. But the fans love to see a bowler gyrate all over the lane, hoping his excited *body English* will in some way result in a strike or spare.

Carmen Salvino is the greatest exponent of this gambit. Whether he is bowling well or not, he puts on a show for the fans, and they flock to see him live and die on every shot.

Sometimes, while I may show no outward emotion, I'm seething inside over my poor performance. I may get angry at myself, but I'll wait until I'm back in the seclusion of my motel room before I let my anger loose. I figure that keeping my temper under control is worth an average of at least three pins a game over a year's time. It could mean more pins for you, depending upon how short a fuse you have.

There is one bowler on tour today—and I'm not going to embarrass him by mentioning his name—who has so much ability he could lead the tour in average every year. But he just can't control his temper. He loses pin after pin because he can't keep his emotions in check.

OK, so you've got a red-hot temper. What can you do to keep it from destroying your game? First, face facts. Every shot just can't be perfect. You must learn to live with imperfection.

Second, take a look around you on the lanes. Look at all those red-faced, wild-eyed, rack-kicking bowlers acting like children. Watch one of them throw the next shot out of the window because of emotional instability.

Third, and most important, think of it this way: if you deliver your best strike ball, you have done all you can do. If somehow,

you didn't get a strike, throw a perfect spare ball. Even if that fails, at least you have tried your best. You can't ask for more. Start all over again on your next ball, chasing the elusive dream of perfection.

COURTESY AND SAFETY

We've talked a lot about the competitive side of bowling, its technical aspects, and the desire and concentration you must maintain to be a good bowler.

But it's my belief that you must also be a courteous bowler or you have missed the point of the game. For me, bowling is a means of making a living. But it must remain a sport, a wonderful competition, or I wouldn't enjoy it.

Whenever you bowl, be it professional, league, or open bowling, always remember that, just as in highway traffic safety, the "driver" on the right has the right of way. Sometimes, you may arrive at the approach and be ready to bowl ahead of the bowler on your right. But if there is any question of who goes first, always defer to him.

I think that's the most important of all the rules of bowling etiquette. Always have respect for the bowler on your right.

Don Carter once gave a perfect statement about another rule of bowling. "Your temper and your language should be as controlled as your delivery," he said.

Apply all the body English you want on an important roll. But always stay within the bounds of your lane and try not to disturb a bowler on a nearby lane.

Never slow up the game. You may be having an off night, but if you paw and toe the line and are indecisive before you deliver the ball, you will upset not only yourself but also some of your teammates or opponents.

TO AVOID SMASHED FINGERS . . . always pick up the ball with the palm of your hand held parallel to the ball return.

Don't needle your opponent. It may seem like fun, but if he or she returns the discourtesy, you may find yourself totally distracted—and, believe me, you deserve to be.

Don't rant and rave and blame the equipment for your shortcomings. Bowling equipment is designed to give everyone an equal chance. If you do not make a strike or spare, or get a seemingly impossible leave on a pocket hit, it wasn't the pins, lane, or pinspotter that was at fault. Try to analyze what you did wrong.

Please don't take food or beverage on the lanes. If you want to have a snack or drink, do so behind the bench area. An accidental spill of a drink or sandwich in the bowling area could result in a sticky approach or shoe, which could mean disaster to a bowler.

A few paragraphs should be devoted to how to pick up a ball properly when it comes back from the pit on the ball return. More than one bowler has gotten bruised fingers by picking up the ball carelessly and getting his or her hand crushed by another ball coming up the return. A 16-pound object can cause a lot of pain when it strikes unsuspecting fingers.

Always be aware of the balls as they come back on the return. When your ball arrives, reach for it with palms held parallel to the ball return. Then if a ball should somehow come up the return when you are not expecting it, that ball will strike your ball, not your fingers or hand.

If you encounter a sticky approach, by all means ask a lane maintenance man to clean it up or apply a powdered wax to rectify the problem. You can save a wrenched knee or back.

Avoid clowning on the lanes. Live it up in team spirit. But don't compromise another bowler's game by irrational actions in the heat of competition.

CONDITIONING AND PRACTICE

I've already said that some of the skinniest, fattest, most ungraceful people can be good bowlers. But if you strive to be an excellent bowler, you must also be in good physical condition.

The pros bowl hundreds of games a week. If we are to excel, we must be in good shape. Someone once estimated that in the normal course of a weekly tournament, the average pro throws the 16-pound ball down the lanes so often that he actually is lifting and controlling over a ton of weight during each tournament.

I would guess that any out-of-shape, over-weight, smoked-out bowler could throw three games a week in league play without suffering any serious problems with his game.

But if you harbor any thoughts of improving your game or moving on to higher averages, you must keep in some type of physical condition, through abstinence, exercise, or a combination of both.

In bowling, your most important physical feature is your legs. A good and a simple way to keep them in shape is jogging. You don't even have to go out on the road—just jog in place for 15 minutes at home every day.

Don't let cigarettes or liquor become crutches. Some players must have a smoke or drink to calm their nerves before facing the pins. You are only deceiving yourself. Both are depressants and will, if counted on heavily, only throw your game off kilt.

A lot of people feel that bowling, as a recreational sport, doesn't follow the rules of conditioning that govern other major sports. That just isn't true.

I've talked a lot about the constant need for practice if you are to become more than an average bowler. But how do you practice? If you have the time and money to practice, concentrate on your strike ball. A lot of average bowlers will try just shooting at the various pins that give them trouble. When they bowl the next time, they don't get a single situation in which the pin they were practicing is a vital one.

When you are practicing, don't bowl as you would in a game. Concentrate on one phase of your game at a time: foot movement, armswing, release, or follow-through.

Start with your strike ball and don't worry about which pins are left standing. Just try and groove the ball in the pocket with the proper speed and revolutions. Then concentrate on your spare shots. If your timing seems to be off, work on your steps and armswing, forgetting what pins you are toppling.

Dissect your game. Decide what you are doing wrong and concentrate on that. If you can, have a pro or top-notch bowler observe you in practice. He may be able to get you on the right track. Then, by practice, you can master your failings.

The time to work on your game is in the summer months. Don't be experimenting, fouling up your game, and hurting your team during the winter league session, unless you really are in trouble.

Whenever you practice, take one segment of your game at a time. Polish it and perfect it. Then move on to another problem area.

DOs AND DON'Ts

DO use concentration as your most vital weapon.

DON'T ever think negatively.

DON'T rule out superstitions as a bowling aid. They can boost your confidence.

DO develop a game plan in your head. Think strikes.

DO take a deep breath before you bowl if you are feeling nervous.

DO remember that you have a chance to make a spare when your first ball isn't perfect.

DON'T lose your temper. It can cost you many pins.

DO follow the simple rules of courtesy and safety when you are on the lanes.

DO practice regularly and keep yourself in good physical condition.

A FINAL WORD

Well, there it is—just about everything I can tell you about the game of bowling.

If you have followed me this far, you can see that becoming a good bowler is not easy. Concentration, desire, dedication to practice, and constant striving for perfection are paramount to success.

Perhaps you don't want to go into the game to such an extent. To you, I say, fine. Have fun. Bowling is that kind of game. It can be played for thousands, nickels and dimes, or simply for the pleasure of relaxation and entertainment.

Anyway you approach the game, you'll be a big winner.

I hope I've been of some help along the way.

glossary

ABC: American Bowling Congress.

Address position: The starting position, in which the bowler stands facing the pins, ready to begin his delivery. The ball is held waist high, and the feet are placed on the correct spot on the approach.

Alley: An old-fashioned term for the bowling lane.

Anchor: The final player on a team to bowl; usually the team's best player.

Angle: An imaginary line drawn from the bowler's feet at the address position to the pin or pins at which he is shooting.

Approach: The 16-foot area in which the address and delivery are made; the steps taken by the bowler across that area.

Area bowling: The method of bowling toward the target arrows on the lane rather than toward the pins. Also called spot bowling and target bowling.

Baby splits: The 2-7 and 3-10 spare shots.

Backup ball: A ball that goes to the right for right-handers or to the left for left-handers, instead of hooking properly.

Barmaid: A pin obscured by another pin.

Bedposts: The 7-10 split.

Beer frame: A frame in which all the members of a team have made strikes. The first bowler who fails to strike must buy a round.

Bellying: Throwing the ball farther to the right than normal on a lane that is hooking too much.

Big ears: *See* Big four.

Big five: A split that leaves five pins, for example, the 4-7 on the left plus the 6-9-10 on the right.

Big four: The 4-6-7-10 split.

Blind: A predetermined score granted a team for an absent member.

Blocking: Setting up, through the use of oil, an illegal track leading to the strike pocket.

Blow: To miss a spare.

Boards: The strips of wood, approximately one inch wide, that form the lane.

Body English: The unconscious movements of a bowler watching his ball.

Bridge: The distance between the finger holes in the ball.

Brooklyn: A 1-2 pocket hit for a right-hander; a 1-3 hit for a left-hander. The opposite of hitting the strike pocket.

Bucket: The 2-4-5-8 spare for a right-hander; the 3-5-6-9 spare for a left-hander.

Channel: The groove into which the ball drops if it rolls off either edge of the lane. Formerly called the gutter.

Cheesecake: A high-scoring lanes.

Chopping: Hitting the front pin and leaving a pin or pins either to the left or right.

Christmas tree: The 3-7-10 split for right-handers; the 2-7-10 for left-handers.

Cincy: The 8-10 split.

Clean: Striking or sparing in every frame.

Convert: To make a spare.

Count: The number of pins that are added to the bowler's score after a strike or spare.

Creeper: A ball that is rolled slowly.

Cushion: The padded section at the back of the pit behind the pins.

Cutoff: Lack of follow-through.

Dead wood: Fallen pins.

Deflection: The glancing action by the ball after it comes in contact with the pins.

Deuce: A 200 game.

Dodo: A ball that is illegally weighted.

Double: Two strikes in succession.

Double pinochle: The 4-6-7-10 split.

Dummy: *See* blind.

Dutch 200: Shooting a 200 game by alternating strikes and spares.

English: The spin of the ball.

Error: *See* blow.

Fast: A term applied to lanes on which it is difficult to throw a hook.

Fenceposts: The 7-10 split.

Field goal: A shot that misses the 7-10 split by going between the two pins.

Fill: The number of pins toppled after a spare.

Floater: A ball that doesn't go where the bowler wants it to because of lane conditions.

Foul: Sliding over the line at the end of the approach; the penalty is the loss of the points made in the shot.

Frame: A bowler's turn to score. The bowler gets two chances to knock down the pins. Ten frames constitute a game.

Fudging: Slowing a ball down to make it go straighter; putting little lift on the ball.

Full: Term applied to a shot that hits the head pin too high.

Garbage hit: A hit that doesn't hit the strike pocket but results in a strike because of the mixing action of the pins.

Goalposts: The 7-10 split.

Grabbing: The action taken by the ball when it begins to hook.

Graveyard: A low-scoring lanes.

Greek church: The 4-6-7-8-10 split.

Groove: A depression in the lane. *See* track.

Gutter shot: Shooting the ball down the outside of the lane, on the edge of the channel.

Handicap: Pins added to an actual score to equalize competition.

Head pin: The 1-pin.

Heads: The area between the foul line and the target arrows located 15 feet down-lane.

High board: A board that has risen on a lane and that hinders the progress of the ball.

Hole: The strike pocket; a split.

Hook: A ball that curves to the right for a right-hander or to the left for a left-hander. The most efficient ball for rolling strikes.

House: Bowling lanes.

Juice: The oil used in lanes conditioning.

Kegler: A bowler.

Key pin: The pin closest to the bowler on a spare shot.

Kickback: The side boards outside the channel off of which the pins may bounce.

Kindling: Lightly weighted pins.

Lane(s): The area on which one bowls; the bowling house.

Laying out the ball: Rolling the ball smoothly onto the lane, without bouncing.

Lazy-10: A 10-pin that wobbles before it falls.

Leave: The pins remaining after the first ball.

Lift: The spin accomplished by pulling the fingers out of the ball upon release.

Lofting: Throwing the ball too far down-lane.

Love tap: A ball that trips the 6-pin into the gutter, where the pin stands momentarily before topping lazily to knock down the 10-pin.

Maples: An old-fashioned word for pins.

Mark: A strike or a spare.

Miss: *See* blow.

Mixing action: The action of the pins on a well-thrown ball. The pins ricochet off each other, causing the greatest possible number of pins to fall.

Mother-in-law: The 7-pin.

Mule ears: The 7-10 split.

Murphy: The 2-7 or 3-10 splits.

Nose dive: Hitting the head pin head-on.

Open frame: A frame without a strike or spare.

Picket fence: The 1-2-4-7 or 1-3-6-10 spares.

Pinboy: A person who set up pins by hand before machines for this purpose were invented.

Pinching: Gripping the ball too firmly.

Pit: The area into which the pins fall.

Pocket: The strike target; between the 1- and 3-pins for right-handers and the 1- and 2-pins for left-handers.

Point of release: The point at which the fingers let go of the ball, rolling it lightly onto the lane.

Poison ivy: The 3-6-10 spare.

Post position: A position of the sliding foot at release, in which the foot points slightly in the direction of the hook.

Rack: A normal setup of 10 pins, before the first ball is thrown.

Rail: A split; sometimes, the 1-2-4-7 or 1-3-6-10 spares.

Rolling out: Failing to hit the strike pocket.

Rug jerker: A 5-pin that is swept out to the right on a strike ball as if someone had jerked a rug out from under it.

Runway: The approach area.

Scratch: A bowler's actual score without a handicap.

Sleeper: A pin hidden from view by another pin.

Slots: High-scoring lanes.

Solid 10: An apparent strike shot that leaves the 10-pin because the 6-pin flies out and around, missing the 10.

Sour apple: The 5-7-10 split.

Span: The distance between the thumb and finger holes on a bowling ball.

Spare: Knocking over all 10 pins in two rolls; the pins remaining after the first roll.

Split: A situation that occurs when the bowler knocks down the head pin and at least one more pin between two or more pins that remain standing.

Spot: A target arrow on a lane; the number of pins awarded a team on handicap.

Straight ball: A ball that goes straight instead of hooking.

Strike: Knocking down all ten pins on the first roll.

Striking out: Bowling three strikes in the tenth frame.

Sweeper: A ball that appears to sweep the pins off the lane.

Tap: A situation in which one pin is left upright on what appears to be a perfect hit. The pin remaining is usually the 7- or 10-pin.

Target: The spot on the lanes toward which the ball is aimed. The target in area bowling will be an arrow on the lane.

Telephone poles: The 7-10 split.

Tilt 10: A situation in which the 6-pin nicks the 10 and makes it fall.

Track: A groove or depression in the lane, caused by wear.

Trip: A pin that ricochets off the side wall and knocks down another pin. The term is usually used when the 4-pin is felled in such a manner.

Turkey: Three straight strikes.

Wall shot: A shot in which pins bounce off the sideboards and cause a strike.

Washout: The 1-2-10 or 1-2-4-10 split for right-handers; the 1-3-7 or 1-3-6-7 for left-handers.

Woolworth: The 5-10 split.

index